D1453112

THE SCRIPTURE ON THE EXPLICATION
OF UNDERLYING MEANING

BDK English Tripiṭaka 25-IV

THE SCRIPTURE ON THE EXPLICATION OF UNDERLYING MEANING

Translated from the Chinese of Hsüan-tsang
(Taishō Volume 16, Number 676)

by

John P. Keenan

Numata Center
for Buddhist Translation and Research
2000

First Printing, 2000
ISBN: 1-886439-10-9
Library of Congress Catalog Card Number: 99-75932

Published by
Numata Center for Buddhist Translation and Research
2620 Warring Street
Berkeley, California 94704

Printed in the United States of America

0306 00/3378Z 5

A Message on the Publication of the English Tripiṭaka

The Buddhist canon is said to contain eighty-four thousand different teachings. I believe that this is because the Buddha's basic approach was to prescribe a different treatment for every spiritual ailment, much as a doctor prescribes a different medicine for every medical ailment. Thus his teachings were always appropriate for the particular suffering individual and for the time at which the teaching was given, and over the ages not one of his prescriptions has failed to relieve the suffering to which it was addressed.

Ever since the Buddha's Great Demise over twenty-five hundred years ago, his message of wisdom and compassion has spread throughout the world. Yet no one has ever attempted to translate the entire Buddhist canon into English throughout the history of Japan. It is my greatest wish to see this done and to make the translations available to the many English-speaking people who have never had the opportunity to learn about the Buddha's teachings.

Of course, it would be impossible to translate all of the Buddha's eighty-four thousand teachings in a few years. I have, therefore, had one hundred thirty-nine of the scriptural texts in the prodigious Taishō edition of the Chinese Buddhist canon selected for inclusion in the First Series of this translation project.

It is in the nature of this undertaking that the results are bound to be criticized. Nonetheless, I am convinced that unless someone takes it upon himself or herself to initiate this project, it will never be done. At the same time, I hope that an improved, revised edition will appear in the future.

It is most gratifying that, thanks to the efforts of more than a hundred Buddhist scholars from the East and the West, this monumental project has finally gotten off the ground. May the rays of the Wisdom of the Compassionate One reach each and every person in the world.

NUMATA Yehan
Founder of the English

August 7, 1991   Tripiṭaka Project

Editorial Foreword

In January 1982, Dr. NUMATA Yehan, the founder of the Bukkyō Dendō Kyōkai (Society for the Promotion of Buddhism), decided to begin the monumental task of translating the complete Taishō edition of the Chinese Tripiṭaka (Buddhist Canon) into the English language. Under his leadership, a special preparatory committee was organized in April 1982. By July of the same year, the Translation Committee of the English Tripiṭaka was officially convened.

The initial Committee consisted of the following members: (late) HANAYAMA Shōyū (Chairperson); BANDŌ Shōjun; ISHIGAMI Zennō; KAMATA Shigeo; KANAOKA Shūyū; MAYEDA Sengaku; NARA Yasuaki; SAYEKI Shinkō; (late) SHIOIRI Ryōtatsu; TAMARU Noriyoshi; (late) TAMURA Kwansei; URYŪZU Ryūshin; and YUYAMA Akira. Assistant members of the Committee were as follows: KANAZAWA Atsushi; WATANABE Shōgo; Rolf Giebel of New Zealand; and Rudy Smet of Belgium.

After holding planning meetings on a monthly basis, the Committee selected one hundred thirty-nine texts for the First Series of translations, an estimated one hundred printed volumes in all. The texts selected are not necessarily limited to those originally written in India but also include works written or composed in China and Japan. While the publication of the First Series proceeds, the texts for the Second Series will be selected from among the remaining works; this process will continue until all the texts, in Japanese as well as in Chinese, have been published.

Frankly speaking, it will take perhaps one hundred years or more to accomplish the English translation of the complete Chinese and Japanese texts, for they consist of thousands of works. Nevertheless, as Dr. NUMATA wished, it is the sincere hope of the Committee that this project will continue unto completion, even after all its present members have passed away.

It must be mentioned here that the final object of this project is not academic fulfillment but the transmission of the teaching of the

Buddha to the whole world in order to create harmony and peace among humankind. To that end, the translators have been asked to minimize the use of explanatory notes of the kind that are indispensable in academic texts, so that the attention of general readers will not be unduly distracted from the primary text. Also, a glossary of selected terms is appended to aid in understanding the text.

To my great regret, however, Dr. NUMATA passed away on May 5, 1994, at the age of ninety-seven, entrusting his son, Mr. NUMATA Toshihide, with the continuation and completion of the Translation Project. The Committee also lost its able and devoted Chairperson, Professor HANAYAMA Shōyū, on June 16, 1995, at the age of sixty-three. After these severe blows, the Committee elected me, Vice President of Musashino Women's College, to be the Chair in October 1995. The Committee has renewed its determination to carry out the noble intention of Dr. NUMATA, under the leadership of Mr. NUMATA Toshihide.

The present members of the Committee are MAYEDA Sengaku (Chairperson); BANDŌ Shōjun; ISHIGAMI Zennō; ICHISHIMA Shōshin; KAMATA Shigeo, KANAOKA Shūyū, NARA Yasuaki, SAYEKI Shinkō, TAMARU Noriyoshi; URYŪZU Ryūshin; and YUYAMA Akira. Assistant members are WATANABE Shōgo and UEDA Noboru.

The Numata Center for Buddhist Translation and Research was established in November 1984, in Berkeley, California, U.S.A., to assist in the publication of the BDK English Tripiṭaka First Series. In December 1991, the Publication Committee was organized at the Numata Center, with Professor Philip Yampolsky as the Chairperson. To our sorrow, Professor Yampolsky passed away in July 1996, but thankfully Dr. Kenneth Inada is continuing the work as Chairperson. This text is the nineteenth volume to be published and distributed by the Numata Center. All of the remaining texts will be published under the supervision of this Committee, in close cooperation with the Translation Committee in Tokyo.

MAYEDA Sengaku
Chairperson
Translation Committee of
the BDK English Tripiṭaka

June 28, 1999

Publisher's Foreword

The Publication Committee works in close cooperation with the Editorial Committee of the BDK English Tripiṭaka in Tokyo, Japan. Since December 1991, it has operated from the Numata Center for Buddhist Translation and Research in Berkeley, California. Its principal mission is to oversee and facilitate the publication in English of selected texts from the one hundred-volume Taishō Edition of the Chinese Tripiṭaka, along with a few major influential Japanese Buddhist texts not in the Tripiṭaka. The list of selected texts is conveniently appended at the end of each volume. In the text itself, the Taishō Edition page and column designations are provided in the margins.

The Committee is committed to the task of publishing clear, readable English texts. It honors the deep faith, spirit, and concern of the late Reverend Doctor NUMATA Yehan to disseminate Buddhist teachings throughout the world.

In July 1996, the Committee unfortunately lost its valued Chairperson, Dr. Philip Yampolsky, who was a stalwart leader, trusted friend, and esteemed colleague. We follow in his shadow. In February 1997, I was appointed to guide the Committee in his place.

The Committee is charged with the normal duties of a publishing firm—general editing, formatting, copyediting, proofreading, indexing, and checking linguistic fidelity. The Committee members are Diane Ames, Eisho Nasu, Koh Nishiike, and the president and director of the Numata Center, Reverend Kiyoshi S. Yamashita.

Kenneth K. Inada
Chairperson
Publication Committee

June 28, 1999

Contents

Contents

Translator's Introduction

The Scripture on the Explication of Underlying Meaning (*Saṃdhi-nirmocana-sūtra*) is a foundational text in the development of Yogācāra thinking in India. It was apparently composed in the second century C.E.[1] It ranks as the initial source for much basic Yogācāra thinking, because it presents the first Yogācāra attempt to develop a hermeneutic for interpreting the Prajñāpāramitā (Perfection of Wisdom) literature.

The Prajñāpāramitā scriptures signaled the arising of Mahayana Buddhism and presented a thoroughgoing critique of the conceptualist approach of the earlier Abhidharma philosophical schools. The writers of the Prajñāpāramitā works deny the validity of any conceptualist understanding of doctrine, seeing such conceptual understanding as fabrication (*prapañca*). Their stress was upon the immediacy of wisdom (*prajñā*) in emptiness (*śūnyatā*) and its validation in practice (*pāramitā*) rather than in analysis.

The Yogācāra masters inherited this mystical approach of the Prajñāpāramitā texts. However, they did not reject the validity of theoretical Abhidharma. Rather they attempted to construct a critical understanding of the consciousness that underlies all meaning, both mystical and theoretical. Their focus was on doctrine, but as it flowed from the practice of meditative centering (*yoga*), rather than as it was understood in acts of conceptual apprehension. In contrast to the Prajñāpāramitā texts' negation of all theory in favor of emptiness, the Yogācārins championed the validity of theory in the context of emptiness.

It was the need to affirm both the mystical thrust of the Prajñāpāramitā and the theoretical approach of the Abhidharma that seems to have led to the doctrine of *The Scripture on the Explication of Underlying Meaning*.

1

There are three distinct themes in this scripture. After the introduction in Chapter One, Chapter Two presents the first theme, a discourse on ultimate meaning (*paramārtha*) in the style of the Prajñāpāramitā texts. That meaning is not to be analyzed by differentiating one concept from another. All words and ideas are nothing but inventions and validate nothing real, for all things are empty of any essence (*svabhāva*) that might support their analytical apprehension.

Yet it was felt that there was a need for verbal expositions of doctrine. Indeed, the Prajñāpāramitā texts are themselves such verbal expositions of the meaning of the Buddha's teachings. The initial Yogācārins had then to evolve a method to affirm both the central, ultimate validity of mystical insight and the conventional validity of verbal explanation. The second theme consists in the development of a critical understanding of the consciousness that expresses itself in both mystical insight and verbal theory.

Chapters Three to Five outline this critical understanding. Chapter Three lays the basic foundation in its description of the nature of the container consciousness (*ālaya-vijñāna*) and its relationship to thinking and perception. Chapter Four then turns to an explanation of the three characteristic patterns in which consciousness functions. The basic interdependent (*paratantra*) nature of consciousness is explained as evolving toward illusory verbal imagining (*parikalpita*), but yet capable of being converted (*āśraya-parivṛtti*) to the full perfection of awakening (*pariniṣpanna*). This understanding allows one to describe the imagined pattern as empty, while assigning a conventional validity to paratantric understanding, once it has been converted from clinging to those imaginings. Chapter Five then applies this formulation of the three patterns of consciousness to an understanding of the essential no-essence of all things, i.e., to the Prajñāpāramitā notion of emptiness. The constant point is that all clinging to imagined essences is empty of meaning and illusory.

In this context the passage on the three turnings of the wheel of doctrine is presented. Here the underlying intent (*saṃdhi*) not only of Hinayana teaching but also of the Prajñāpāramitā scriptures is presented as in need of explication, for their meaning has to be drawn out (*neyārtha*) through the fully explicit (*nitārtha*) hermeneutic of the previous analysis of consciousness.

Chapters Six to Eight present the third theme, the implications of this understanding of consciousness for practice. Chapter Six treats centering (*yoga*), from which the previous insights have been elicited. Its two moments of quietude and vision reflect the central concern with mystical insight, with the conventional expression of ineffable truth. Chapter Seven describes the bodhisattva stages and the six perfections (*pāramitā*s). The eighth (and final) chapter concentrates upon the wisdom activity of a Tathāgata and includes an explanation of the meaning of scripture (*sūtra*), discipline (*vinaya*), and theory (*mātṛkā*), thus ending the scripture with an analysis of theory and reasoning.

Throughout, the hermeneutic employed seeks to make explicit (*nirmocana*) the underlying meaning and intent (*saṃdhi*) of the Buddha as enunciated in previous Mahayana texts. *The Scripture on the Explication of Underlying Meaning* is then the initial Yogācāra presentation of a critical understanding of the genesis of meaning within consciousness, and constitutes the basic hermeneutic for the subsequent thought of Asaṅga and Vasubandhu.

There are two Western-language translations. The first is a French rendering entitled *Saṃdhinirmocana Sūtra: L'explication des Mystères* by Étienne Lamotte (Paris: Adrien Maisonneuve, 1935). The second is an English translation entitled *Wisdom of Buddha: The Samdhinirmocana Sūtra* by John Powers (Berkeley, CA: Dharma Publishing, 1995). Both are careful and intelligent translations. Both include the Tibetan text.

The brief notes included at the end of this translation are meant not to unpack the history or exegesis of terms, but merely to help situate the reader unfamiliar with the movement of Yogācāra thought within its broader themes and agendas.

THE SCRIPTURE ON THE EXPLICATION
OF UNDERLYING MEANING

Chapter I

Thus Have I Heard

Thus have I heard. At one time the World-honored One was dwelling in an immeasurable abode adorned with seven gems that shone brilliantly and emitted a great light illuminating all the immeasurable world realms. Its limitless regions were brilliantly adorned and well arranged. They had no boundaries. Their quantity was beyond reckoning, and they surpassed anything found in the triple world. Having been brought forth from good roots, that abode transcended this world. It was characterized by a pure conscious construction of perfect mastery. It was the domain of Tathāgatas. Like clouds, great bodhisattvas gathered together there. An immeasurable number of gods, *nāga*s, *yakṣa*s, *gandharva*s, *asura*s, *garuḍa*s, *kiṃnara*s, *mahoraga*s, humans, nonhumans, and similar beings were in attendance. There the great taste of the doctrine sustained their delight and happiness and brought about all benefit for sentient beings. It had destroyed the oppressive, defiled inclinations of passion, and it was far removed from all inimical forces. Surpassing all adornments was the adorned abode of the Tathāgata. Its paths were the cultivation of great recollection and wisdom. Its vehicles were great quietude and vision. Its entry doors were the great liberations of emptiness, imagelessness, and desirelessness. It was ornamented with a multitude of good qualities. It was established by the multitude of the great, jeweled flower king.

In that great palace, the World-honored One's entirely purified understanding did not appear as dual. He entered into the unmarked doctrine. He dwelled in the Buddha abode, realized the equality of all Buddhas, and reached the state of no obstacles. The irreversible teaching of the doctrine he propounded was unhindered. That which he established was inconceivable. Traversing the three times in the reality of equality, his bodies issued forth to all world realms. His wisdom had no uncertainty in regard to anything. He had perfected his great enlightenment in all practices. His wisdom had no doubt in regard to anything. All the bodies he manifested could not be differentiated. His wisdom, which was well sought after by all the bodhisattvas, had attained that victorious far shore of a Buddha's nondual abode. That unified wisdom of the Tathāgata's liberation was indeed ultimate. He had realized the equality of Buddha lands. He reached to the reality realm. He exhausted space and would never come to an end.

He was accompanied by an immeasurable multitude of great word-hearers, all of whom were docile sons of the Buddha. Their thinking was well liberated. Their understanding was well liberated. Their discipline was well purified, and they had set their aim upon joy in doctrine. They had heard much, and retained and

688c accumulated what they had heard. They thought good thoughts, spoke good words, and did good deeds. Their wisdom was swift, quick, incisive, salvific, penetrating, great, expansive, unequaled. Having perfected that wisdom gem, they were endowed with the three knowledges of remembering former lives, of the divine eye, and of the destruction of contaminants. They had attained the happiness of the highest state in the present world. They dwelled in the field of pure merit. Their deportment was tranquil and in no way imperfect. The perfection of their great patience and gentleness was without decrease. Already good, they revered and practiced the holy teachings of the Tathāgata.

Also present were an immeasurable number of great bodhisattvas, assembled from various Buddha lands. All dwelled in the great vehicle [Mahayana] and roamed in the doctrine of that great vehicle. Their minds maintained equality in regard to all sentient beings. They were free from discriminating time from the end of time. They had suppressed all inimical forces. They were far removed from the thinking of all the word-hearers and individually enlightened ones. They were sustained by the joy and happiness of that great, expansive taste of the doctrine. They had risen above the five dreads and had assuredly entered the state of no-returning. Appearing before them, they mitigated the oppressive lands that torment sentient beings. The principal ones were named the Bodhisattva Gambhīrārthasaṃdhinirmocana, the Bodhisattva Vidhivatparipṛcchaka, the Bodhisattva Dharmodgata, the Bodhisattva Suviśuddhimati, the Bodhisattva Viśālamati, the Bodhisattva Guṇākara, the Bodhisattva Paramārthasamudgata, the Bodhisattva Āryāvalokiteśvara, the Bodhisattva Maitreya, and the Bodhisattva Mañjuśrī.[2]

Chapter II

The Descriptive Marks of the Truth of Ultimate Meaning

At that time the Bodhisattva Vidhivatparipṛcchaka questioned the Bodhisattva Gambhīrārthasaṃdhinirmocana, in the presence of the Buddha, and said: "Son of the Victor, it is said that all things are not dual. What does 'all things' mean? And why are they not dual?"

The Bodhisattva Gambhīrārthasaṃdhinirmocana answered the Bodhisattva Vidhivatparipṛcchaka and said: "Good son, in sum, all things are of two kinds, conditioned and unconditioned. Herein conditioned things are neither conditioned nor unconditioned, and unconditioned things are neither unconditioned nor conditioned."

The Bodhisattva Vidhivatparipṛcchaka again questioned the Bodhisattva Gambhīrārthasaṃdhinirmocana and said: "Son of the Victor, what does it mean to say that conditioned things are neither conditioned nor unconditioned or that unconditioned things are neither unconditioned nor conditioned?"

Gambhīrārthasaṃdhinirmocana addressed the Bodhisattva Vidhivatparipṛcchaka and said: "Good son, the term 'conditioned' is a provisional word invented by the First Teacher. Now, if it is a provisional word invented by the First Teacher, then it is a verbal expression apprehended by imagination. And if it is a verbal expression apprehended by imagination, then, in the final analysis, such an imagined description does not validate a real thing. Therefore, the conditioned does not exist. Good son, the term 'unconditioned' is also invented from language [and it also validates nothing real].[3]

"Furthermore, besides the conditioned and the unconditioned, any other expression that exists in language is the same. But, it might be objected, is it not true that there are no expressions without some [corresponding] reality? What, then, is the reality here? I would reply that it is that reality apart from language and realized in the perfect awakening of the saints through their holy wisdom and insight apart from all names and words. It is because they desire to lead others to realize perfect awakening that they provisionally establish [such expressions] as 'the conditioned' as verbal descriptions.[4]

"Good son, the term 'unconditioned' is also a word provisionally invented by the First Teacher. Now, if the First Teacher provisionally invented this word, then it is a verbal expression apprehended by imagination.[5] And, if it is a verbal expression apprehended by imagination, then, in the final analysis, such an imagined description does not validate a real thing. Therefore, the unconditioned does not exist. Good son, the term 'conditioned' is also invented from language [and it validates nothing real].

"Besides 'the unconditioned' and 'the conditioned,' any other expression that exists in language is the same. But [some may object], is it not true that there are no expressions without some [corresponding] reality? What then is that reality here? I would reply that it is that reality apart from language and realized in the perfect awakening of the saints through their wisdom and insight apart from all names and words. It is because they desire to lead others to realize perfect awakening that they establish [such expressions] as 'the unconditioned' as verbal descriptions."

Then the Bodhisattva Vidhivatpariprcchaka again questioned the Bodhisattva Gambhīrārthasaṃdhinirmocana and said: "Son of the Victor, why is it that those saints, being freed from language through holy wisdom and insight, realizing perfect awakening in that ineffable nature of reality, and desiring to lead others to realize perfect awakening, provisionally establish verbal descriptions, such as 'conditioned' and 'unconditioned'?"

The Bodhisattva Gambhīrārthasaṃdhinirmocana addressed the Bodhisattva Vidhivatpariprcchaka and said: "Good son, one can liken [those saints] to skillful magicians or apprentices, who,

689a

setting themselves up at a crossroads, make things like broken tiles, grass, leaves, pieces of wood, etc., appear to be magical things, [such as] herds of elephants, horses, chariots, soldiers, gems, pearls, 689b cat's-eyes, conches, crystal, coral, treasure, grain, storehouses, etc. Some people, dull and slow-witted, of perverse understanding and lacking acumen, see and hear those magical things and think that they really are elephants, horses, etc. They tenaciously cling to the verbal expressions that are engendered from what they themselves have seen and heard, [thinking] only that is true and real and everything else is false. It is only later that they are forced to change their opinions. Other people, not dull nor slow-witted, of good understanding and having acumen, see and hear those magical things and understand that what they see are not really elephants, horses, etc., but rather magical tricks that confuse the eye and cause it to engender the concept of a herd of elephants, the imagined concept of a herd of horses, the many imagined concepts of grain, storehouses, or other magical illusions. They do not tenaciously cling to verbal expressions that are engendered from what they have seen and heard. With them it is not the case that only that is true and real and everything else is false. But, in order to express objects [seen and heard], they also follow the accepted language. Afterwards they do not have to reconsider.

"In like manner, some sentient beings, foolish and profane, have not yet attained to the transcendent understanding of the saints and are not able to recognize that in all things reality is apart from language. After they have seen and heard about all conditioned and unconditioned [things], they think that what they have learned is most certainly really existing conditioned and unconditioned things. They cling tenaciously to the verbal expressions engendered by what they have seen and heard. Only that is true and everything else is false. But later they must reconsider.

"Other sentient beings, not foolish, who have gained insight into the holy truth, who have attained the transcendent insight of the saints, do truly understand that in all things reality is apart from language. After they have seen and heard about conditioned

13

and unconditioned things, they think that what they have learned are most certainly not really existing conditioned and unconditioned things. Rather they are descriptions engendered from imagination and are magical, confused understandings in which one produces concepts about the conditioned and the unconditioned, concepts about whether they exist or not. They do not tenaciously cling to verbal expressions that are engendered from what they have seen and heard or think that only [those expressions] are true and everything else false. [But,] in order to express the meanings they know, they follow the accepted language. Afterwards they are not forced to reconsider. Thus, good son, the saints, being freed from language through their holy wisdom and insight in this regard, realize the perfect awakening that reality is truly apart from language. It is because they desire to lead others to realize perfect awakening that they provisionally establish names and concepts and call things conditioned or unconditioned."

689c

At that time the Bodhisattva Gambhīrārthasaṃdhinirmocana recited these verses to emphasize his meaning:

> Buddha speech is apart from language and is nondual. Its depths are beyond the sphere of fools. In their idiotic confusion, fools delight in duality and rely upon verbal fabrications.[6] Whether without understanding or with perverse understanding, they will revolve in the suffering of transmigration for a great length of time. They are indeed far from the discourse of true wisdom and will certainly be reborn as cows, sheep, and so forth.

At that time the Bodhisattva Dharmodgata addressed the Buddha and said: "World-honored One, at a distance from this eastern sector equal to the sands of seventy-two Ganges, there is a world realm named Viśālakīrti, whose Tathāgata is named Viśālakīrti Tathāgata. I used to live there before I came here. In that Buddha land I once saw seventy-seven thousand heretics together with their teachers gathered in one place to consider the descriptive marks of the ultimate meaning of all things. But although they thought, pondered, investigated, and thoroughly examined these marks of the ultimate meaning of all things, in the end they were unable to reach any conclusion. They went no further than to exclude certain interpretations, delineating and modifying their own interpretations. They confronted one another and argued fiercely. Their mouths emitted barbed comments, pointed, captious, angry, vicious; and then each went his separate way. I then thought to myself, 'The appearance of a Tathāgata in the world is indeed a rare occurrence. But, because of his appearance, it becomes possible to understand the marks of ultimate meaning, which transcend the sphere of any reasoning.'"[7]

Then the World-honored One addressed the Bodhisattva Dharmodgata and said: "Good son, it is just as you have expressed it. I am perfectly awakened to the marks of the truth of ultimate meaning, which transcend any reasoning. Being already perfectly awakened, I declare, preach, explain, teach, and illumine [those marks] for others. Why do I do this? Because I have preached that ultimate meaning is realized internally by each saint, while reasoning is attained in the give and take [of joint discussion] among common worldlings. Dharmodgata, from this principle you should understand that ultimate meaning transcends the descriptions of reasoned meaning. Furthermore, Dharmodgata, I have preached 690a that ultimate meaning does not function through images, but the functioning of reason does move within the realm of images. From this principle, Dharmodgata, you should understand that ultimate meaning transcends the descriptions of reasoned meaning. Furthermore, Dharmodgata, I preach that ultimate meaning is ineffable, but the functioning of reason moves within the realm of language. From this principle, Dharmodgata, you should understand that ultimate meaning transcends the descriptions of reasoned meaning. Furthermore, Dharmodgata, I teach that ultimate meaning severs all expression, but the functioning of reason moves within the realm of expression. From this principle, Dharmodgata, you should understand that ultimate meaning transcends the descriptions of reasoned meaning. Furthermore, Dharmodgata,

I preach that ultimate meaning severs all disputation, but the functioning of reason does move within the realm of disputation about meaning. From this principle, Dharmodgata, you should understand that ultimate meaning transcends the descriptions of reasoned meaning.

"Furthermore, Dharmodgata, you should understand that it is like a man who all his life long was accustomed to tart and bitter tastes. He would be incapable of comprehending, evaluating, or appreciating the wonderful taste of honey or rock candy. It is like a man who for ages has placed his concern upon and taken his delight in cravings [for this or that]. With his desires burning like fire, he would be unable to comprehend, evaluate, or appreciate the wonderful inner detachment that severs the images of all sense objects, sounds, smells, tastes, and touches. It is like a man who for ages has placed his concern upon and taken his delight in fine, worldly conversations. He would be unable to comprehend, evaluate, or appreciate the joy of the inner, holy silence of tranquility. It is like a man who for ages has placed his concern upon and taken his delight in all the worldly ideas he had heard, expressed, and understood. He would be unable to comprehend, evaluate, or appreciate the final cessation that forever eradicates all ideas and destroys personality.[8] Understand, Dharmodgata, it is like a man who for ages has placed his concern upon and taken his delight in worldly disputation. He would be unable to comprehend, evaluate, or appreciate the fact that in north Kuru [where I have preached] there are no disputes over the constituents or over no-self. In like fashion, Dharmodgata, reason is entirely unable to comprehend, evaluate, or appreciate the descriptive marks of ultimate meaning, which transcend the functioning of any reasoning."

At that time the World-honored One recited these verses to emphasize his meaning:

> The sphere that is internally realized without descriptions cannot be spoken and severs expressions. Ultimate meaning, laying to rest all disputes, transcends all the descriptive marks of reasoning.

At that time the Bodhisattva Suviśuddhimati addressed the Buddha and said: "Wonderful it is, World-honored One, that I have been able to hear these words of yours. It is just as you have said, for the marks of the truth of ultimate meaning, being subtle and profound, can be characterized as neither identical with nor different from all things. They are indeed difficult to fathom.[9] World-honored One, I once saw an assembly of bodhisattvas gathered together and seated. They were in the stage of fully cultivating their commitment, and were all considering the descriptive marks of the truth of ultimate meaning, whether they were identical with or different from the descriptive marks of conditioned states of being. Some of these bodhisattvas said that there was no difference between the marks of the truth of ultimate meaning and the marks of conditioned states of being. Others said that it was not true that there was no difference between the marks of the truth of ultimate meaning and the marks of conditioned states of being, but that the marks of the truth of ultimate meaning do differ from the marks of conditioned states of being. Yet other bodhisattvas, in doubt and perplexed, said: 'Which bodhisattvas are speaking truth and which falsity? Which are reasoning intelligently and which not intelligently?' But, whether they declared that the marks of ultimate meaning did not differ from the marks of conditioned states of being, or that the marks of ultimate meaning did differ from the marks of conditioned states of being, I, World-honored One, thought to myself that all these good sons were foolish and slow-witted. They did not have insight, and, behaving poorly, did not reason intelligently in regard to the subtlety and profundity of the truth of ultimate meaning, for it transcends being characterized as either identical with or different from conditioned states of being and cannot be so understood."

690b

Then the World-honored One addressed the Bodhisattva Suviśuddhimati and said: "Good son, it is just as you have expressed it. All those good sons were indeed foolish and slow-witted. They did not have insight, and, behaving poorly, did not reason intelligently in regard to the subtlety and profundity of the truth of ultimate meaning, for it does transcend being characterized as either identical with or different from conditioned states of being. Why is this so, Suviśuddhimati? It is because one cannot comprehend the descriptive marks of the truth of ultimate meaning in names by performing such exercises.

690c "Why is this so, Suviśuddhimati? It is because, if the descriptive marks of the truth of ultimate meaning were not different from conditioned states of being at all, then at this very moment all common worldlings would have already gained insight into truth. They all necessarily would have already attained the quiescent cessation of supreme skill or would have realized full, perfect awakening. But, [on the other hand,] if the descriptive marks of ultimate meaning were entirely different from the marks of conditioned states of being, then those who have already gained insight into truth would not have expunged images of conditioned states of being. And if they had not expunged images of conditioned states of being, then they would not have attained liberation from bondage to those images. Not being liberated from those images, they would not be freed from bondage to their gross weaknesses. Not being freed from bondage to gross weaknesses, those who have gained insight into truth would have been unable to attain the quiescent cessation of supreme skill or full, perfect awakening. But, Suviśuddhimati, it is not the case that at this very moment all the common worldlings have already gained insight into truth, are already capable of attaining the quiescent cessation of supreme skill, or have realized full, perfect awakening. Therefore the opinion that the descriptive marks of the truth of ultimate meaning are not different from the descriptive marks of conditioned states of being is not reasonable. If someone were to say that the descriptive marks of the truth of ultimate meaning were not different from the descriptive marks of conditioned states of being, from this above argument you should understand that this opinion is neither intelligent nor truly reasonable.[10] Suviśuddhimati, neither is it the case that those who have gained insight into truth have not been able to expunge all the images of conditioned states of being, for they have indeed been able to expunge them. It is not the case that those who have gained insight into truth have been incapable of liberation from bondage to the images of conditioned states of being, for they have indeed been capable of such liberation. It is not the case that those who have gained insight into truth have been incapable of liberation from bondage to gross weaknesses, for they have indeed been capable of such liberation. It is precisely because they have been capable of liberation from these two obstacles that they have been able to attain the quiescent cessation of supreme skill and to realize full, perfect wisdom. Therefore, the opinion that the descriptive marks of the truth of ultimate meaning are entirely different from the descriptive marks of conditioned states of being is not reasonable. If some say that the marks of the truth of ultimate meaning are entirely different from the marks of conditioned states of being, from the above argument you should understand that this opinion is neither intelligent nor truly reasonable.

"Moreover, Suviśuddhimati, if the marks of the truth of ultimate meaning were identical with the marks of conditioned states of being, then, just as the marks of conditioned states of being are defiled, so also the marks of the truth of ultimate meaning would be defiled. Suviśuddhimati, if the marks of the truth of ultimate meaning were entirely different from the marks of conditioned states of being, then the common mark that describes conditioned states of being could not be termed the mark of the truth of ultimate meaning. But, Suviśuddhimati, the descriptive marks of the truth of ultimate meaning are not defiled, and the common marks of conditioned states of being are termed the mark of the truth of ultimate meaning. Therefore it is not reasonable to say that the descriptive marks of the truth of ultimate meaning are identical with the descriptive marks of conditioned states of being, nor that they are entirely different one from the other. From this argument you should understand that both those who speak for the identity of marks and those who speak for their complete difference are neither intelligent nor reasonable.

"Moreover, Suviśuddhimati, if the descriptive marks of ultimate truth were identical with the descriptive marks of conditioned states of being, then, just as the mark of the truth of ultimate meaning is undifferentiated in all conditioned states, so all the marks of those conditioned states would be undifferentiated. Then those who practice meditation would not have to search for ultimate meaning in all the conditioned states of being that they have seen, heard, understood, and known. On the other hand, if the descriptive mark of the truth of ultimate meaning were entirely different from conditioned states of being, then it would not be true that all conditioned states of being are manifestations only of the absence of self, of the absence of essence. The marks of ultimate truth would then simultaneously be held to be characterized in two different manners, one of defilement and one of purity. But, Suviśuddhimati, these marks of conditioned things are indeed different. Those who practice meditation do search for ultimate meaning in the conditioned states of being they have seen, heard, understood, and known. Also, all conditioned states of being are indeed manifestations only of the absence of self, the absence of essence, and they are rightly termed marks of ultimate truth. It is not true that it is simultaneously characterized in two manners, one of defilement and one of purity. Therefore, the opinion that the marks of the truth of ultimate meaning are either identical with or entirely different from the marks of conditioned states of being is not reasonable. If some say that these marks of the truth of ultimate meaning are either identical with or entirely different from the marks of conditioned states of being, from this argument you should understand that they are neither intelligent nor truly reasonable.

"It is like unto the fresh white color of a conch shell, for it is not easily ascertained whether [that color] is identical with or different from the shell. The yellow color of gold presents a similar case. Or consider the melodies from the sound of a guitar, for it is difficult to ascertain whether that sound is identical with or different from the guitar. Or take the fragrance that wells up from aloes, for it is difficult to tell whether it is identical with or different from the aloes. Or take the bitter taste of pepper, for it is difficult to tell if it is identical with or different from the pepper. A similar case is the insipid taste of an astringent nut. It is like the silky skin of a moth and its softness, for it is difficult to ascertain if that silky texture is identical with or different from the softness. Or take the rich liquor on the top of boiled butter. Is it identical with or different from the boiled butter?

"Likewise it is difficult to tell whether impermanence is identical with or different from conditioned states of being, whether suffering is identical with or different from impure states of mind, whether the no-self of personality is identical with or different from all things, whether inquietude is identical with or different from covetousness. The same is true about anger and delusion vis-à-vis covetousness. Thus, Suviśuddhimati, the descriptive marks of the truth of ultimate meaning cannot be said to be either identical with or different from the descriptive marks of conditioned states of being. Suviśuddhimati, I have perfectly understood the descriptive marks of the truth of ultimate meaning, which are subtle indeed, profound indeed, hard to fathom indeed, which transcend all descriptions as being identical with or different from all things. Having perfectly understood, I declare, preach, explain, and illumine for the sake of others." 691b

Then the World-honored One recited these verses to emphasize his meaning:

> The descriptive marks of the realm of conditioned states of being and of ultimate meaning are apart from being described either as identical or as different. If one imagines them to be either identical or different, one is acting unreasonably. Because of bondage to images and to gross weaknesses, sentient beings must assiduously cultivate quietude and vision, and then they will be able to attain liberation.

At that time the World-honored One addressed the venerable Subhūti and said: "Subhūti, in the world of sentient beings, how many do you know who cherish their pride and in a prideful manner state their understanding? And how many do you know who state their understanding without pride?"

The venerable Subhūti addressed the Buddha and said: "World-honored One, in the world of sentient beings, I know a few who state their understanding without pride, but I know innumerable, untold sentient beings who cherish their pride and state their understanding in a prideful manner. World-honored One, once I was dwelling in a grove in a forest. A large number of monks lived nearby. I saw them assemble after sunrise to discuss various issues and to propose their understandings, each according to his insight.

"Some proposed their understanding of the aggregates, their descriptive marks, their arising, their exhaustion, their destruction, and the realization of their destruction. Others, in like fashion, proposed their understanding of the [twelve] bases [of consciousness] and of dependent co-arising, while yet others proposed their understanding of sustenance, its descriptive marks, arising, exhaustion, destruction, and the realization of its destruction. Yet others proposed their understanding of truth, its descriptive marks, the full awareness of truth, the severance [brought about by] truth, the realization of truth, and the cultivation of 691c truth. Others proposed their understanding of the realms, their descriptive marks, their various natures, their multiplicity, their destruction, and the realization of their destruction. Others proposed their understanding of the stations of recollection, their descriptive marks, the states they are able to control, their cultivation, their arising from a state of being non-arisen, their assured non-forgetfulness after arising, and their increase from repeated practice. At the same time, others proposed their understanding of true severance, of the supernatural abilities, of the sense faculties, of the powers, of the factors of awakening, while yet others talked about the eightfold path, its descriptive marks, the states it is able to control, its arising from a state of being non-arisen, its assured unforgettableness once it has arisen, and its increase from repeated practice.

"World-honored One, when I saw them, I thought that all those venerable persons were engaged in addressing these various issues and proposing their interpretations, each according to the insights he had attained. But, note well, all of them cherished their pride and, because they clung to that pride, they were unable to comprehend the one universal taste of the truth of ultimate meaning. But you, World-honored One, have already explained that the descriptive mark of the truth of ultimate meaning is rare, most subtle indeed, most profound, difficult to fathom. You have explained that one universal taste as difficult to fathom. World-honored One, if practicing monks find it difficult to fathom this one universal taste of the truth of ultimate meaning in this holy teaching, then how much harder will it be for heretics to understand it?"[11]

Then the World-honored One addressed Subhūti and said: "This is so, Subhūti, for I have been awakened to the truth of ultimate meaning which is of one universal taste, most subtle, most profound, most difficult to fathom. Having been awakened, I declare, preach, explain, and illumine it for the sake of others. What is it that I have preached, Subhūti? I have preached that the purified content of understanding in all the aggregates is the truth of ultimate meaning. I have preached that the purified content of understanding in all dependent co-arising, in sustenance, in the realms, in recollection, in true severance, in the supernatural abilities, in the factors of awakening, and in the factors of the path is the truth of ultimate meaning.[12] This purified content of understanding is characterized as being of one taste, being undifferentiated in all the aggregates, in all the bases, in all they discussed [above], for it is of one taste and not differentiated. It is from this principle that the truth of ultimate meaning is of one universal taste.

"Furthermore, Subhūti, once those practicing monks who cultivate centering have understood the suchness of a single group [of questions], the selflessness of the teaching on ultimate meaning, then they will not engage in analyzing one after the other the aggregates, bases, dependent co-arising, sustenance, truth, the

692a

realms, recollection, true severance, the supernatural abilities, the faculties, the powers, the factors of awakening, or the factors of the path. The selflessness of the teaching of suchness and ultimate meaning is based upon the nondual wisdom of suchness and ultimate meaning. They then will come to awareness and realize the truth of ultimate meaning, which is of one universal taste. Therefore, Subhūti, from this principle understand that the truth of ultimate meaning is of one universal taste.

"Furthermore, Subhūti, if, like all the aggregates, like all the bases, dependent co-arising, sustenance, truth, realms, recollection, true severance, supernatural abilities, sense faculties, powers, factors of awakening, and factors of the path, all of which are described by differentiating one from the other; if, like these, suchness, ultimate meaning, and no-essence had descriptive marks that differentiated one from the other, then these would issue from causes, they would be caused. And, if they arose from causes, they would themselves be conditioned. And, if conditioned, they would not be ultimate meaning. And, if they were not ultimate meaning, then one would once more have to seek the truth of another ultimate meaning. It is because suchness, ultimate meaning, and the no-essence of all things are not said to be caused, do not arise from causes, and are not conditioned that they are the truth of ultimate meaning. Once one attains this ultimate meaning, there is no further need to seek another ultimate meaning. Only it is eternal and permanent, whether a Tathāgata appears in the world or not, for in all things reality is established, the reality realm perdures. Therefore, Subhūti, from this principle you should understand that the truth of ultimate meaning is of one universal taste.

"Subhūti, in empty space there are differences in the multiple varieties of color, while [space itself] remains unmarked, undifferentiated, and unchanged by them. Rather it encompasses all those marks within its one taste. In a similar fashion, the truth of ultimate meaning is in all things, which are of different natures and do have differing marks; and it encompasses all those marks with its one taste."[13]

Then the World-honored One recited these verses to emphasize his meaning:

Encompassing all marks with one taste, ultimate meaning is taught by all Buddhas to be undifferentiated. If one were to discriminate it in those differentiations, one should assuredly be foolish and prideful.

Chapter III

The Descriptive Marks of Mind, Thought, and [Sense] Consciousness

At that time the Bodhisattva Viśālamati addressed the Buddha and said: "World-honored One, you have spoken about bodhisattvas skilled in the secrets of mind, thought, and [sense] consciousness. 692b Why do you speak of these bodhisattvas as being skilled in the secrets of mind, thought, and [sense] consciousness? What do you mean by describing them in this fashion?"

Then the World-honored One addressed the Bodhisattva Viśālamati and said: "It is very good, Viśālamati, that you are able to question the Tathāgata about this profound theme. You raise this question because you desire to benefit and gladden unlimited sentient beings, because you have compassion for the world and all its gods, men, angels, and so forth, so that they may be led to realize meaning, benefit, and happiness. Attend, then, and I will explain the meaning of the secrets of mind, thought, and [sense] consciousness.

"Viśālamati, you should understand that sundry sentient beings fall into sundry destinies in their transmigrations through the six destinies. Whether egg-born, womb-born, moisture-born, or magically born, they issue from birth. From the very first instant [of their births], the maturation, evolution, unification, increase, and growth of their minds, together with all their seeds, depend upon two appropriations. The first is their appropriation of the material senses in the body. The second is their appropriation of the propensity toward verbal fabrication in discriminating

27

images and words. In the worlds of form, [sentient beings] have these two appropriations, but not in the world of no-form.[14]

"Viśālamati, this consciousness is also termed the appropriating consciousness, because it is taken up together with the body. It is also termed the receptacle consciousness, because this consciousness joins itself to and lies hidden [in that body] in a common security and risk. It is also termed mind, because this consciousness mines and accumulates material forms, sounds, odors, tastes, and touches.[15]

"Viśālamati, because the appropriating consciousness is the support and ground, there evolves the group of the six consciousnesses of seeing, hearing, smelling, tasting, touching, and thinking. The conditions that produce visual consciousness are the eye and material forms. In synergy with such visual consciousness, there evolves a thinking consciousness that simultaneously discriminates those very objects [seen]. The conditions that elicit aural, olfactory, gustatory, and tactile consciousness are the ear, nose, tongue, and body, together with sound, odor, taste, and touch. In synergy with these aural, olfactory, gustatory, and tactile consciousnesses there evolves a thinking consciousness that simultaneously discriminates these same objects.

"Viśālamati, when a single visual consciousness evolves, at that very instant a discriminative thinking consciousness arises in synergy with that visual consciousness. When two, three, four, or five consciousnesses develop, at that very instant a discriminative thinking consciousness arises in synergy with those same five consciousnesses.[16]

"Viśālamati, it is like a great rush of flowing waters. If the conditions for one wave are present, only one wave will develop. If the conditions for two or more are present, then many waves will develop. But that great rush of waters itself flows on constantly without interruption or cessation. It is also like the surface of a very pure mirror. If the conditions for one image are present, then only one image will appear [in that mirror]. If the conditions for two or more images are present, then many images will appear.

692c

28

But the mirror surface does not alter itself into the image and suffers no change at all. Likewise, Viśālamati, the appropriating consciousness is similar to those rushing waters, for it is the support and ground. When the conditions for the arising of a single visual consciousness are present, then a single visual consciousness develops. When the conditions for the arising of the five sense consciousnesses, or however many, are present, then those consciousnesses develop.

"Viśālamati, although in this fashion the bodhisattvas, supported upon the wisdom of abiding in doctrine, are skilled in the secrets of mind, thought, and sense consciousness, yet it is not on this account that the Tathāgata described them as skilled in mind, thought, and sense consciousness. Viśālamati, all those bodhisattvas are said to be skilled in ultimate meaning and are described by the Tathāgata as skilled in ultimate meaning because each one within himself does not see appropriation as though it were real, does not see appropriating consciousness, nor storing, nor the receptacle consciousness, nor accumulation, nor mind, nor visible forms nor visual consciousness, nor sounds nor aural consciousness, nor odors nor olfactory consciousness, nor taste nor gustatory consciousness, nor touch nor tactile consciousness [as though they were real]. They do not see objects of thought nor thinking consciousness [as though real]. Viśālamati, it is on this account that they are called bodhisattvas skilled in the secrets of mind, thought, and sense consciousness, and are so described by the Tathāgata."

Then the World-honored One recited these verses to emphasize his meaning:

The appropriating consciousness is profound and subtle indeed; all its seeds are like a rushing torrent. Fearing that they would imagine and cling to it as to a self, I have not revealed it to the foolish.[17]

Chapter IV

The Characteristic Patterns of All Things[18]

At that time the great Bodhisattva Guṇākara addressed the Buddha and said: "World-honored One, you have spoken about bodhisattvas skilled in the characteristic patterns of all things. Why do you so speak of them? Why do you describe them so?"

Then the World-honored One addressed the Bodhisattva Guṇākara and said: "It is excellent, Guṇākara, that you have been able to question the Tathāgata about this profound theme. You bring forth this question because you desire to benefit and gladden unlimited sentient beings, because you have compassion for the world with all its gods, men, angels, and so forth, so that they might be led to attain meaning, benefit, and happiness. Attend and I will explain the marks of all things for you.

"In sum, the marks of all things are threefold. The first is the characteristic pattern of clinging to what is entirely imagined. The second is the characteristic pattern of other-dependency. The third is the characteristic pattern of full perfection.

"The pattern of clinging to what is entirely imagined refers to the establishing of names and symbols for all things and the distinguishing of their essences, whereby they come to be expressed in language. The pattern of other-dependency refers to the pattern whereby all things arise co-dependently: for if this exists, then that exists, and if this arises, then that arises. This refers to [the twelvefold conditions, starting with] 'conditioned by ignorance are karmic formations,' [and ending with] 'conditioned by origination is this grand mass of suffering,' [the last of the twelve conditions].

31

The pattern of full perfection refers to the universally equal suchness of all things. Bodhisattvas penetrate to this suchness because of their resolute zeal, intelligent focusing, and true reflection. By gradually cultivating this penetration, they reach unsurpassed true awakening and actually realize perfection.

"Good son, the pattern of clinging to what is entirely imagined is like the defective vision of one who has cataracts in his eyes. The pattern of other-dependency is like those deceptive images in the confused vision of the one with the cataracts, for they appear to be distinct images, such as hairs, flies, small particles, or patches of different colors. The pattern of full perfection is like the unconfused objects seen by the pure vision of one with sound eyes and no cataracts.

693b

"Good son, it is just as when a pure crystal comes into contact with and is tinted with the color blue, it appears to be a blue sapphire or a blue gem. Because it takes on the appearance of a blue sapphire or a blue gem, it confuses sentient beings. When it comes into contact with the color red, it appears to be a ruby and so confuses sentient beings. When it comes into contact with the color green, it appears to be an emerald and so confuses sentient beings. When it comes into contact with the color yellow, it seems to be gold and so confuses sentient beings. Similarly, Guṇākara, just as those tinted colors appear upon the pure crystal, so the propensity toward language of the characteristic pattern of clinging to what is imagined is superimposed upon the other-dependent pattern. Just as upon that pure crystal one falsely clings to blue sapphires, rubies, emeralds, or gold, so upon the other-dependent pattern of consciousness one clings to the imagined, for that other-dependent pattern is like the crystal. Just as, when in a constant and continual fashion the pure crystal no longer has any images of sapphires, rubies, emeralds, or gold, it is without [their] reality or essence, so when the pattern of other-dependency no longer has imagined images in it, it is also in fact without [their] reality or essence, and is then the pattern of full perfection.

"Furthermore, Guṇākara, the imagined pattern can be understood as caused by the interplay between images and words. The

32

other-dependent pattern can be understood as caused by the grasping of those imagined images upon that other-dependent pattern. The pattern of full perfection can be understood as caused by the absence of grasping the imagined pattern upon the other-dependent pattern.

"If bodhisattvas are truly able to understand the imagined   693c pattern as it arises upon the other-dependent pattern in all things, they then will be truly able to understand all things as unmarked. If bodhisattvas are truly able to understand the other-dependent pattern [of their consciousness], they then will be truly able to understand all things as defiled. If bodhisattvas are truly able to understand the fully perfected pattern, they then will be truly able to understand all things as purified. If bodhisattvas truly understand all things as unmarked in the other-dependent pattern, they then will be able to abandon defiled things. If they are able to abandon defiled things, they will be able to realize things as purified. In this fashion, Guṇākara, since they truly understand all three patterns [of consciousness], they will truly know things as unmarked, defiled, and purified. Because they abandon defiled things, they will realize things as purified. And this is why those bodhisattvas are described by the Tathāgata as skilled in the characteristic patterns of all things."

Then the World-honored One recited these verses to emphasize his meaning:

> If one does not understand things as unmarked, one will be unable to abandon defiled things. Not being able to abandon defiled things, one will obstruct the realization of wondrously purified things. Not gaining insight into the sinfulness of all one's actions, one will be wild, sinful, and injurious to sentient beings. Sadly enmeshed in transient things, are not such people lost and pitiable?[19]

Chapter V

The Absence of Essence

At that time the great Bodhisattva Paramārthasamudgata addressed the Buddha and said: "World-honored One, once when I found myself alone in a quiet place, I thought to myself: 'The World-honored One in an immeasurable number of sermons has explained the aggregates, their specific characteristics, their arising, their destruction, their abandonment, their full understanding. In like fashion he has explained the bases of consciousness, dependent co-arising, and sustenance. In an immeasurable number of sermons, he has explained the [four] truths, their specific characteristics, full understanding, abandonment, and the practices that lead to their realization. In an immeasurable number of sermons, he has explained all the realms, their specific characteristics, varieties, differentiation, nondifferentiation, abandonment, and full understanding. In an immeasurable number of sermons, he has explained the stations of recollection, their specific characteristics, the act of controlling [mental states], which [states] are controlled, how by meditation what has not yet arisen can be produced, how what has already arisen can be maintained, their unforgettableness, repeated practice, growth, and increase. And just as he has explained the stations of recollection, so he has explained true abandonment, the supernatural abilities, the sense faculties, the factors of awakening. In an immeasurable number of sermons, he has explained the eightfold holy path, its specific characteristics, the act of controlling [states of mind], which [states] are thus controlled, how by meditation what has not yet arisen can be produced and what has already arisen can be maintained, its unforgettableness, repeated practice, growth, and increase.'

"World-honored One, you also have explained that all things have no-essence, no arising, and no passing away, are originally quiescent, and are essentially in cessation. I do not know what to make of this, World-honored One. With what implicit intent did you explain that things have no-essence, no arising, and no passing away, are originally quiescent, and are essentially in cessation? I wish to question the Tathāgata about this. I pray that the Tathāgata will deign to explain what his underlying intent was in saying this."

Then the World-honored One addressed Paramārthasamudgata and said: "Excellent indeed, Paramārthasamudgata, your thinking is indeed intelligent. Excellent indeed, good son, that you have been able to question the Tathāgata concerning this profound theme. You raise this question because you desire to benefit and gladden immeasurable sentient beings, for you have compassion for the world and all its gods, men, angels, etc., so that they may be led to attain meaning, benefit, and happiness. Attend and I will explain my underlying intent in saying that all things have no-essence, no arising, no passing away, are originally quiescent, and are essentially in cessation.

"Paramārthasamudgata, you should understand that, in reliance upon the three kinds of no-essence, I have explained that all things whatsoever have no-essence, for descriptive marks have no-essence, arising has no-essence, and ultimate meaning has no-essence. Good son, descriptive marks have no-essence, for all things are characterized by imaginative clinging. This is so because it is names and symbols that establish those marks, and there is no inherent characteristic in things. This then is what I call the no-essence of marks. The arising of things has no-essence, for all things arise in dependence upon others. This is so because they depend upon the causal power of others and do not arise from themselves. Therefore this is what I call the no-essence of arising. The ultimate truth of all things has no-essence, for, from their arising, all things have no-essence. This is what I call the no-essence that is identical with the conditioned arising of things. I also call it the no-essence of ultimate meaning because I preach that among all things, that realm of the purified content of understanding is to be regarded as the no-essence of ultimate meaning. The characteristics of the other-dependent pattern of consciousness are not, however, themselves this realm of the purified object of understanding. Therefore I call this the no-essence of ultimate meaning. Moreover, that fully perfected pattern of all things I also term the no-essence of ultimate meaning, for the absence of selfhood in all things whatsoever I call ultimate meaning, or no-essence, because this is the truth of ultimate meaning, because it is manifested by the absence of essence. For these reasons I call it the no-essence of ultimate meaning. 694b

"Good son, flowers in the sky are like the essential no-essence of descriptive marks. The arising of magical images is like the essential no-essence of arising, as well as one aspect of the essential no-essence of ultimate meaning. Just as empty space is manifested everywhere by the absence of material forms, so is the other aspect the essential no-essence of ultimate meaning, which is manifested everywhere by the absence of selfhood in all things.

"Good son, this is my underlying intent about the three kinds of essential no-essence whereby I have preached that all things have no-essence. Paramārthasamudgata, you should understand that it was with this underlying intent about the essential no-essence of marks that I preached that all things have no arising and no passing away, are originally quiescent, and are essentially in cessation.[20] For if the descriptive marks of things do not exist in themselves, then they do not arise. If they do not arise, then they do not pass away. If they do not pass away, then they are originally quiescent. If they are originally quiescent, then they are essentially in cessation, for herein there is not the slightest part that could be led once again into final cessation. Therefore, with this underlying intent concerning the essential no-essence of marks, I have preached that all things have no arising and no passing away, are originally quiescent, and are essentially in cessation. Good son, it was with this underlying intent about the essential no-essence of ultimate truth manifested through the no-self of

things that I preached that all things have no arising and no passing away, are originally quiescent, and are essentially in cessation. This no-essence of ultimate meaning manifested through the
no-self of things is for all times and forever, because the reality
nature of all things abides in an unconditioned state and is not
associated with any of the defilements. Because at all times and
forever the reality nature of all things abides, it is unconditioned.
Because it is unconditioned, it has no birth and no passing away.
Because it is not yoked to any of the defilements, it is originally
quiescent and essentially in cessation. Therefore, with this underlying intent concerning the no-essence of ultimate meaning manifested by the absence of selfhood in things, I have preached that
all things have no birth and no passing away, are originally quiescent, and are essentially in cessation.

"Moreover, Paramārthasamudgata, I am not propounding
these three kinds of no-essence because among the varieties of
sentient beings in the world, some regard the pattern of imaginative clinging as a distinct essence, or because they regard the pattern of other-dependency or the pattern of full perfection as distinct
essences. Rather it is because sentient beings superimpose the
pattern of imaginative clinging over that of other-dependency and
694c   full perfection that I propound these three kinds of no-essence.[21]
Sentient beings, because they imagine there are essences and
characteristics to be clung to in the other-dependent and fully perfected patterns, produce language about this and that. To the degree that they produce language, they cling to images of essences
in the other-dependent and fully perfected patterns because their
minds are permeated with language, their understanding follows
upon language, their inclinations are toward language. Thus they
cling to various imagined essences and characteristics in their
other-dependent and fully perfected patterns of consciousness. And,
clinging to such in those patterns, they cling to the imagined pattern. Therefore they will bring forth their other-dependent pattern
in future [lives]. Defiled by passion, actions, and birth, they will
gallop about in transmigration for a long time. For a long time

they will circle about without surcease and experience suffering, whether in the hells, among animals, among ghosts, in the heavens, among angels, or among men.[22]

"Moreover, Paramārthasamudgata, I preached the teaching on the essential no-essence of arising for all those sentient beings who have not yet planted roots of goodness, who have not yet purified themselves from obstacles, who have not yet matured their continuity [of consciousness], who have not yet cultivated liberation, who have not yet been able to accumulate the two requisites of merit and wisdom. When they attend to this teaching, they will partially be able to understand that all conditioned states, which are dependently co-arisen, are impermanent, inconstant, not comforting, grievously transient, and destructive. Then their minds will produce deep dread and detestation for all conditioned states. When this has happened, then they will reject all evil. When they no longer do evil, they will be able to cultivate and practice good. And, practicing good, they will be able to plant roots of goodness not previously planted, they will be able to purify obstacles not previously purified, they will be able to mature their continuities not previously matured. Because of this they will cultivate liberation and accumulate the two requisites of merit and wisdom.

"But even though they plant roots of goodness until they accumulate these two requisites of merit and wisdom, yet in the essential no-essence of arising, they will not really be able to understand the essential no-essence of marks and the two kinds of essential no-essence of ultimate meaning. They will not yet perfectly be able to detest all conditioned states. They will not yet be able to sever their desires or be perfectly liberated. They will not be altogether liberated from the defilements of passion, action, and birth. It is for them that the Tathāgata once more preaches this doctrine on the essential no-essence of marks and the essential no-essence of ultimate meaning. He indeed desires to lead them to be able perfectly to detest all conditioned states, perfectly to sever their desires, perfectly to be liberated, and to transcend the defilements of all passion, action, and birth.

695a

39

"When they attend to this teaching, then in the essential no-essence of arising, they will be perfectly able to believe and understand the essential no-essence of marks and ultimate meaning. They will ponder, think, and really understand, for in their other-dependent pattern of consciousness, they will cling to no imagined essences or marks. Because of a wisdom not permeated by language, because of an insightful wisdom not formed by language, because of a wisdom freed from inclinations toward language, they will be able to destroy the pattern that arises dependent upon others, for, sustained by the wisdom power of this teaching, they will eternally be able to sever all causes for future [rebirths] forever. Because of this they will be able to detest all conditioned states, they will be able to sever all their desires and be perfectly liberated. They will be able to be entirely liberated from the three defilements of passion, action, and birth.

"Moreover, Paramārthasamudgata, because they follow this path, all those sentient beings who belong to the word-hearers' vehicle will realize unsurpassed, quiescent cessation, as will all those who belong to the solitary enlightenment vehicle or to the Tathāgata vehicle. For all word-hearers, solitary enlightened ones, and bodhisattvas, this is the one wondrous path of purification. This is the one ultimate purification. There is no other. It is with this underlying intent that I have preached that there is only one vehicle. It is not that in the world of sentient beings there are not sentient beings of various different lineages, for some are slow to understand, some are not so slow, and some are quick to understand.[23]

"Good son, a person of the word-hearers' lineage, turned toward quiescence, even if he were to be skillfully led by the energetic perseverance of all the Buddhas, would yet be unable to be led to sit upon the wisdom seat and realize full, supreme awakening. This is so because from their origin they possess only an inferior lineage, because their compassion has been weak, because they have lived in fear of suffering. Since their compassion has been weak, they have turned their backs upon deeds that benefit and gladden all sentient beings. Since they have lived in fear of suffering, they have turned their backs upon engendering any conditioned activities. I have never taught that one who turns his back upon deeds to benefit and gladden all sentient beings, who turns his back upon engendering conditioned activities, will sit upon the wisdom seat and realize supreme awakening. Therefore I teach that such persons are termed word-hearers totally intent upon quiescence. 695b

"But if a person of the word-hearers' lineage were to turn toward wisdom, I would identify him as a bodhisattva. This is so because, having already been liberated from the obstacle of passion, when he receives the universal awakening of all Tathāgatas his mind will also be liberated from the obstacle to knowing.[24] Because initially [such a person] was intent upon his own benefit, the intensity of his practices liberated him from the obstacle of passion, and therefore the Tathāgata designated him as belonging to the lineage of the word-hearers.

"Moreover, Paramārthasamudgata, sentient beings have various commitments both to the doctrinal discipline I have well presented and to the doctrine of the good teaching enunciated by my fully purified intent. But a Tathāgata relies upon the three kinds of essential no-essence; and with such a profound intent he has presented a summary of that doctrine when he preached the scriptures of implicit meaning, saying that all things have no-essence and no arising, are originally quiescent, and are essentially in cessation, for such are their hidden and profound marks.[25]

"If then sentient beings, who have already planted roots of superior goodness, who have already been purified from all obstacles, who have already matured the continuities [of their consciousness], who have already repeatedly cultivated liberation, who have already been able to accumulate the requisites of superior merit and wisdom, if such were to attend to the doctrine of these scriptures [of implicit meaning], they would truly understand the underlying intent of my words and would engender a deep faith in and understanding of this doctrine, for they would truly penetrate this meaning in an infallible understanding. Relying upon the practices of that penetration, they would quickly be able to realize the final stage. Because of their deeply engendered pure faith in me, they would know that the Tathāgata is supremely awakened and manifests true wisdom in all things.

"There are [other] sentient beings of upright disposition, who have already planted roots of superior goodness, who have already been purified from all obstacles, who have already matured the continuities [of their consciousness], who have already repeatedly cultivated liberation, but who are yet unable to accumulate the requisites of superior merit and wisdom. Although [they have] such upright dispositions, they lack the ability thoughtfully to make judgments on [doctrinal] propositions. Yet, because they do not set up their own views, when they attend to this doctrine, even though they lack the ability truly to understand the underlying intent of my words, yet they will be able to engender a deep faith in this teaching. They will believe in this scripture: 'The teaching of the Tathāgata is a most profound revelation, is associated with the most profound emptiness, is difficult to glimpse, difficult to understand, is beyond thinking, is not within the sphere of rational reflection, is to be subtly interpreted, is understood [only] by the wise.' But they abide in it with humility and say: 'The wisdom of all the Buddhas is profound indeed! The reality of all things is profound indeed! Only the Buddha Tathāgatas are able to understand it well, for it is not something we are able to understand. For the sake of sentient beings of various commitments, all the Buddha Tathāgatas have turned the wheel of the true doctrinal teaching, for the wisdom and insight of all Buddha Tathāgatas is infinite, while our wisdom and insight follows in their wake.' Although they are able to revere this scripture and declare it to others, to copy it and protect it, to unroll it and disseminate it, to venerate and honor it, to recite it and review it, yet they will still be incapable of the effort of meditating upon it, and thus they will be incapable of penetrating the underlying intent of my words. But those sentient beings

695c

42

will be able to increase the requisites of merit and wisdom, and they will be able to mature the continuities [of their consciousnesses] that have not been matured.

"There are [other] sentient beings who, just like those [described above], have not yet been able to accumulate the requisites of merit and wisdom, but whose lineages are not of an upright disposition or character. Although they do have the ability to make judgments on [doctrinal] propositions, yet, abiding in their own views, even if they hear this doctrine, they will be unable truly to understand the underlying intent of my words. Even if they were to engender faith and understanding in this doctrine, they would only be clinging to the words that express the meaning, that is: that all things most certainly have no-essence and no arising, are originally quiescent, and are essentially in cessation.[26] Consequently, they take up the view of nihilism and the nonexistence of all marks. With this view of nihilism and the nonexistence of all marks, they negate all marks, for [they think that] everything is [simply] unmarked. They dispense with and negate not only those marks of things clung to in imagination, but also the marks of other-dependency and full perfection. Now, the very ability to designate the imagined pattern presupposes that other-dependency and full perfection are described by marks.[27] If, then, in dispensing with and negating the descriptive marks of the imagined, they regard the marks of other-dependency and full perfection as unmarked, they in fact dispense with and negate all three characteristic patterns. They do form concepts about my teaching, but, in their negation of meaning, they do not form concepts of its meaning. Because, while forming concepts of my teaching, in their negation of meaning, they do not form concepts of its meaning. They do maintain this doctrine, but they do not maintain its meaning. Nevertheless, because they have engendered faith and understanding in regard to this doctrine, their merit will increase, but they will turn away from and lose wisdom because they engender clinging to what is meaningless. Because they turn away from wisdom, they will lose that wide, limitless doctrine. 696a

"Yet other sentient beings listen to them and take their doctrine as the [true] doctrine and their negation of meaning as [true] meaning. If they follow that view, they will form their concept of doctrine from that doctrine and their concept of meaning from that negation of meaning; they will devote themselves to that doctrine as doctrine and to that negation of meaning as meaning. Therefore they likewise will turn away from and lose the good doctrine.

"Other sentient beings do not follow this view, but as soon as they hear that all things have no-essence and no arising, are originally quiescent, and are essentially in cessation, they feel dread. Feeling such dread, they say: 'This is not the teaching of the Buddha, but rather the teaching of a demon.' With such an understanding, they attack and curse this scripture. Therefore they encounter great misfortune and are blocked by the obstacle of their action [against the doctrine]. This is why I have taught that if one forms the view that all descriptive marks are no marks and propounds this meaninglessness as meaning, this will bring about the obstacle of action [against the doctrine]. Because they beguile limitless sentient beings, they cause them also to be blocked by this obstacle of action [against the doctrine].

"Good son, there are other sentient beings who have not yet planted roots of goodness, who have not yet been purified from all obstacles, who have not yet matured their continuities [of consciousness], who have not repeated their commitments, who have not yet accumulated the requisites of merit and wisdom, and whose lineage is not of an upright disposition or character. Even though they are able thoughtfully to judge [doctrinal] propositions, yet they always maintain their own views. Even if they hear this doctrine, they will be unable truly to understand the underlying intent of my words or to have deep faith in this doctrine. They will form the concept that this doctrine is not [true] doctrine and that this meaning is not meaning. Clinging to the idea that this doctrine is not [true] doctrine and that this meaning is not meaning, they publicize their evaluation, saying: 'This is not the teaching of the Buddha, but of a demon.' With such an understanding they slander, reject, curse, and revile this scripture as useless and mistaken; and in untold ways they attack, criticize, and discard this scripture. They regard all those who have faith in this scripture as a rival faction. From the very beginning they are blocked by the obstacle of their action [against doctrine], and thus they impede [others] by means of this obstacle of action [against doctrine]. It is easy to describe the beginning of this obstacle of action and to estimate how many hundreds of thousands of eons it will take for it to be overcome. Good son, these are the differences in the various kinds of commitments of sentient beings to my well-enunciated and well-controlled doctrinal discipline and my good doctrinal teaching expressed with a purified intent."

At that time the World-honored One recited these verses to emphasize his meaning: 696b

All things have no-essence, no arising, and no passing away,
are originally quiescent, and are essentially in cessation.
What wise man speaks thus without an underlying intent?
I have taught the no-essence of marks, arising, and ultimate meaning, but one who does not know the underlying intent of the Buddha will lose the true path and be unable to travel thereon. All those paths of purity and all the purifications rely upon this one [path] only, for there is no second. Thus herein I have established the single vehicle, but this does not mean that there are no differences in the lineages of sentient beings. In the world of sentient beings, unlimited beings simply are delivered in their individual persons and enter quiescence, for it is difficult to attain that cessation realized together with the great compassion and courage that does not turn away from sentient beings. In the uncontaminated realm, subtle and difficult to conceive, liberations are equal and undifferentiated, for [there] all meaning is complete and free from delusion and suffering, without duality or comparison, for this is eternal happiness.

At that time the Bodhisattva Paramārthasamudgata addressed the Buddha and said: "World-honored One, the intent underlying the words of all Buddha Tathāgatas is rare, rare indeed! It is subtle, subtle indeed! It is profound, profound indeed! It is difficult to penetrate, difficult to penetrate indeed! I now understand this meaning enunciated by the World-honored One as follows. The World-honored One has designed [the teaching] so that the marks of all things are essentially without essence in reference to the pattern of clinging to what is imagined, whereby the attribution of names and symbols to conditioned images, that support those imagined descriptive marks clung to within the range of discrimination, are taken to be the aggregate of material form, the descriptive marks of its essence, the descriptive marks of its specific difference, whereby the attribution of [such] names and symbols is taken to be the mark of the essence or difference of the arising of material form, the passing away of material form, or [the complete knowledge] of the eternal severance from material form.

"The World-honored One has designed [the teaching] that the arising of all things is essentially without essence, and one aspect of [the teaching] is that ultimate meaning is essentially without essence in reference to the pattern of other-dependency, which is the conditioned image supporting those imagined descriptive marks clung to within the realm of discrimination. I now understand this meaning enunciated by the World-honored One as follows, for those marks clung to by imagination upon the conditioned images that support such imaginative clinging within the range of discrimination, validate nothing real, and this is their essential nature as no-essence.

"The World-honored One has designed the other aspect of [the teaching] that ultimate meaning is without essence in reference to the pattern of full perfection, the purified content of understanding that is the no-self of things, that is suchness, that is termed the pattern of full perfection. This is how the material aggregate or the other aggregates should be explained. This is how each of the twelve bases should be explained. This is how each of the twelve branches of existence should be explained. This is how each of the four sustenances should be explained. This is how each of the six realms and the eighteen elements should be explained.

"I understand this meaning enunciated by the World-honored One as follows. The World-honored One has designed [the teaching] that the marks of all things are essentially without essence in reference to the pattern of clinging to the imagined, i.e., the fact that the attribution of names and symbols to the conditioned images that support clinging to imagined descriptive marks within the realm of discriminations is taken to be the truth on suffering. The World-honored One has designed [the teaching] that the arising of all things is essentially without essence in reference to the pattern of other-dependency, i.e., those conditioned images that support clinging to imagined descriptive marks within the realm of discrimination. I now understand this meaning enunciated by the World-honored One as follows. Since those conditioned images that support clinging to the imagined within the realm of discrimination validate nothing real, their essence is precisely without essence, for this is the no-self of things, suchness, the purified content of understanding. It is this that is termed the pattern of full perfection. In reference to this, the World-honored One has designed the other aspect of [the teaching] that ultimate meaning is essentially without essence. The other three truths should be explained like this first truth of suffering, as should the stations of recollection, true severance, the supernatural abilities, the sense faculties, the powers, the factors of awakening, and the factors of the path. All these should be explained in this manner.

"I understand this meaning enunciated by the World-honored One as follows. The World-honored One has designed [the teaching] that the marks of all things are essentially without essence in reference to the pattern of clinging to the imagined, i.e., the fact that the attribution of names and symbols to the conditioned images that support clinging to the imagined within the realm of discrimination is taken to be either the essential or the specific mark of true concentration, its ability to control, that which it

696c

must control, its true cultivation to elicit what has not yet been elicited, its strengthening of what has already been elicited, its unforgettableness, its repeated cultivation, its increase, and its expansion. The World-honored One has designed [the teaching] that the arising of things is essentially without essence, and one aspect of [the teaching] is that ultimate truth is essentially without essence in reference to the pattern of other-dependency, i.e., those conditioned images that support clinging to the imagined within the realm of discrimination. I would explain the meaning enunciated by the World-honored One as follows: if, in those conditioned images that support clinging to imagined marks in the realm of discrimination, those marks clung to by imagination validate nothing real, then this is the essence that is essentially without essence, the no-self of things, suchness, the purified content of understanding. It is this that is termed the pattern of full perfection.

"World-honored One, just as dried ginger must be put into the prescriptions of all medicinal powders and elixirs, just so, World-Honored One, the explicit teaching that all things have no-essence, no arising, and no passing away, are originally quiescent, and are essentially in cessation must be put into all the scriptures of implicit meaning. World-honored One, just as pigments pervade all they color with the identical, single hue of their coloring, whether blue, yellow, red, or white, and thus demonstrate that coloring action, just so, World-honored One, the explicit teaching that all things have no-essence, etc., pervades all scriptures of implicit meaning with its identical, single hue, and thus demonstrates the implicit meaning of those scriptures. World-honored One, just as the addition of warm cheese to cooked delicacies like cakes or fruit produces an exquisite taste, just so, World-honored One, the addition of the explicit teaching that all things have no-essence, etc., to scriptures of implicit meaning produces exquisite delight. World-Honored One, just as empty space pervades everywhere with its identical, single flavor and obstructs no activity, just so, World-Honored One, the explicit teaching that all things have no-essence, etc., pervades all scriptures of implicit meaning with its identical,

697a

single flavor and obstructs no activity performed by word-hearers, solitary enlightened ones, or bodhisattvas."

At that time the World-honored One praised the Bodhisattva Paramārthasamudgata and said: "Excellent, excellent it is, good son, that you have been able to understand so well the underlying intent enunciated by the Tathāgata. Also the similes of the dried ginger, the pigment, the warm cheese, and empty space were right to the point. Paramārthasamudgata, it is exactly as [you have explained], not different at all. It is exactly as you have maintained."

At that time the Bodhisattva Paramārthasamudgata addressed the Buddha and said: "In the country of Benares at Ṛṣipatana in the Deer Park, the World-honored One first turned the wheel of doctrine, [teaching] the four holy truths for those setting out in the word-hearers' vehicle. This turning of the wheel was marvelous and wonderful, such as nobody, whether gods or men, had been able to turn in the world before. Nevertheless there were superior teachings, for [this first turning] had to be interpreted and occasioned controversy. Then the World-honored One with an underlying intent turned the wheel for the second time for the sake of those setting out in the great vehicle, [teaching] that all things have no-essence, no arising, and no passing away, are originally quiescent, and are essentially in cessation. This turn- 697b ing of the wheel was marvelous and wonderful indeed. Nevertheless there were teachings superior to this, for it also had to be interpreted and occasioned controversy. The World-honored One then with an explicit meaning for the third time turned the wheel of doctrine for those setting out in all the vehicles, [teaching] that all things have no-essence, no arising, and no passing away, are originally quiescent, and are essentially in cessation. This turning was the most marvelous and wonderful that had ever occurred in the world. It had no superior nor did it contain any implicit meaning nor occasion any controversy.[28]

"World-honored One, if a good son or good daughter, having heard this teaching that all things have no-essence, no arising, and no passing away, are originally quiescent, and are essentially in cessation, with the explicit meaning as it was enunciated by the Tathāgata, were to believe, copy, protect, honor, disseminate, recite, or meditate and reflect upon it, how much merit would they engender through their effort of meditating upon it?"

At that time the World-honored One addressed the Bodhisattva Paramārthasamudgata and said: "Paramārthasamudgata, the merit engendered by that good son or good daughter would be limitless, incalculable, incomparable. I can but suggest a small part of it for you, like a bit of dirt on one's fingernail in comparison to the earth. It does not amount to one-hundredth part, nor one-thousandth part, nor one-hundred-thousandth part. It cannot be reckoned as even the tiniest part. Or it is like the pool in a cow's tracks compared to the waters of the four great oceans, which does not reach one-hundredth part, etc. Such would be the merit attained by hearing and believing and by the effort expended to meditate upon the teaching of the scriptures of implicit meaning. But even this does not come to one-hundredth, not to the tiniest part of the merit attained by hearing and believing and by the effort expended in meditating upon this scripture of explicit meaning."

Then the Bodhisattva Paramārthasamudgata addressed the Buddha and said: "World-honored One, how should we designate this teaching on the explication of underlying intent? How should we reverence it?"

The Buddha answered Paramārthasamudgata and said: "Good
697c son, it is designated the explicit teaching on ultimate meaning, and you should reverence it as such." When this explicit teaching on ultimate meaning was enunciated in the great assembly, six hundred thousand sentient beings produced the mind of supreme awakening, three hundred thousand word-hearers removed themselves far from defilement and pollution and in this doctrine attained the wisdom eye of doctrine, one hundred fifty thousand word-hearers separated themselves definitively from all contaminated states of mind and attained liberation, and seventy-five thousand bodhisattvas attained the patience of the doctrine of no arising.

Chapter VI

The Analysis of Centering

At that time the Bodhisattva Maitreya addressed the Buddha and said: "World-honored One, in the great vehicle, when a bodhisattva practices the meditation of quietude and vision, what is his support? What is his station?"

The Buddha answered: "Maitreya, good son, you should understand that in the great vehicle when a bodhisattva practices the meditation of quietude and vision, his support and station is the conventional exposition of the doctrine and the commitment not to cast off full, supreme awakening."[29]

The Bodhisattva Maitreya addressed the Buddha and said: "The World-honored One has taught [that meditation has] four kinds of content. The first is that content accompanied by images for reflection, the second is that content not accompanied by images for reflection, the third is that content which extends to the limit of the phenomenal, and the fourth is that content which fulfills duty. Among these four which is the content of quietude? Which the content of vision? And which is the content of both together?"

The Buddha answered the Bodhisattva Maitreya and said: "Good son, the single content of quietude is not accompanied by an image for reflection. The single content of vision is accompanied by an image for reflection. The double content of both together is the limit of phenomenal reality and the fulfillment of duty."

The Bodhisattva Maitreya addressed the Buddha and said: "World-honored One, how is the bodhisattva able to seek quietude and to be well trained in vision by supporting himself upon these four kinds of contents of quietude and vision?"

The Buddha answered the Bodhisattva Maitreya and said: "Good son, the conventional exposition of the doctrine as I have enunciated it for bodhisattvas consists in the scriptures, the metrical verses, the prophecies, the hymns, the discourses, the narratives, the parables, the apothegms [of the Buddha], the accounts of previous lives, the extensive discourses, the accounts of miracles, and the expositions. Bodhisattvas listen attentively and accept these [teachings] docilely. With their words well understood, their ideas well considered, their views well clarified, alone in a forested place they focus their thought upon the doctrines they have heard and pondered, for they are now capable of thinking reflectively upon those doctrines. In the continuity of their inner minds they focus and reflect, and repeatedly abide in this correct practice. They place their bodies and their minds at ease. This is what is termed quietude, and this is the quietude bodhisattvas seek. With their body and mind at ease, while abandoning the [ordinary] modalities of thinking, they thoroughly examine and understand that doctrine upon which they have so well reflected in the images brought about by concentration. In those meanings known through the images brought about by inner concentration, they are able to correctly investigate and examine, to ponder and search out everything, whether patience, happiness, wisdom, views, or awakening. It is this that is termed vision, and this is how bodhisattvas are able to be well trained in insight."

The Bodhisattva Maitreya addressed the Buddha and said: "World-honored One, if the bodhisattvas internally reflect upon and think about the mind without having yet attained ease of body and mind, what do you call that type of reflection?"

The Buddha answered the Bodhisattva Maitreya and said: "Good son, that is not the reflection of quietude at all! Rather it is a reflection concomitant with the commitment to quietude."

"World-honored One, if the bodhisattvas, not having yet reached ease of body and mind, attentively reflect upon images as the content of inner concentration in accord with the doctrines upon which they have reflected, what is that type of reflection called?"

[The Buddha answered:] "Good son, that is not the focusing of quietude at all! Rather it is a reflection concomitant with the commitment leading to quietude."

The Bodhisattva Maitreya addressed the Buddha and said: "World-honored One, are the paths of quietude and vision to be described as different or identical?"

The Buddha addressed the Bodhisattva Maitreya and said: "Good son, they are to be described as neither different nor identical. They are not different because their objective is the content known in vision. They are not identical because images for reflection are not the objective [of quietude]." 698b

The Bodhisattva Maitreya addressed the Buddha and said: "World-honored One, are the images brought forth by all concentrations and vision to be described as different from or identical with thinking?"

The Buddha answered the Bodhisattva Maitreya and said: "Good son, they must be described as identical with thinking. This is so because those images are nothing but ideas. Good son, I have taught that the object of consciousness is nothing but a manifestation of conscious construction only."[30]

"World-honored One," [Maitreya asked,] "if those images brought about in this manner are identical with thinking, then how can thinking reflect back and look upon itself?"

"Good son," [the Buddha answered,] "nothing ever looks at anything.[31] Rather, when thinking occurs as such or such, then such and such images make their appearance. Good son, when a well polished and cleaned surface of a mirror encounters a material shape, it reflects the underlying material thing and we say [not only] that we see the image [but that, distinct from the material thing], the image appears as an object. In this manner, when thought arises, it seems to differ from the images that appear in concentration."

"World-honored One, all the images that sentient beings have, which occur because their minds encounter material form, etc., present themselves as distinct essences. Are these [images] identical with thinking?"

"Good son, they are indeed identical, even though, with their mistaken awareness, the foolish are unable truly to understand that these images are nothing but conscious constructions and consequently misunderstand them."

The Bodhisattva Maitreya addressed the Buddha and said: "World-honored One, how can we describe the single-minded practice of vision of the bodhisattvas?"

The Buddha answered the Bodhisattva Maitreya and said: "Good son, by continuously focusing, they reflect only upon the images of thinking."

"How then," [Maitreya asked,] "World-honored One, can we describe the single-minded practice of quietude of the bodhisattvas?"

"Good son," [the Buddha answered,] "by a continuous focusing they reflect only upon thinking uninterrupted [by images]."

"World-honored One, how then can we describe the joint practice of quietude and vision of the bodhisattvas?"

"Good son, they correctly reflect upon the focusing on one point."

"World-honored One, what then are the images of thinking?"

"Good son, they are the images for reflection brought about by concentration, the content of vision."

"World-honored One, what is thinking uninterrupted [by images]?"

"Good son, it is the objective of quietude, the thinking which encounters those images."

"World-honored One, how does thought focus thinking upon one point?"

"Good son, it is the understanding that all of the images in concentration are nothing but conscious construction, or, having already understood this, the reflecting upon suchness."

The Bodhisattva Maitreya addressed the Buddha and said: "World-honored One, what are the varieties of vision?"

The Buddha answered the Bodhisattva Maitreya and said: "Good son, in sum, there are three kinds. The first is vision from images. The second is vision from inquiry. The third is vision from penetration. Vision from images is that vision which reflects solely

upon images for reflection brought about by concentration. Vision
from inquiry is that vision which through wisdom attentively
reflects upon those things not yet well understood in order to understand them well. Vision from penetration is that vision which
attentively reflects upon those things already well understood
by encompassing them within wisdom in order to realize them and
attain liberation."

The Bodhisattva Maitreya addressed the Buddha and said:
"World-honored One, what are the general varieties of quietude?"

The Buddha answered the Bodhisattva Maitreya and said:
"Good son, since they follow upon that thinking uninterrupted [by
images], you should understand that here also there are three
kinds. There are also eight kinds, for each meditation is a kind of
quietude, from the first to the [eighth meditation] of neither
conceptualization nor nonconceptualization. Again there are four
kinds, for each of the four immeasurable activities of friendli-
ness, compassion, joy, and abandonment is a kind of quietude."

The Bodhisattva Maitreya addressed the Buddha and said:
"World-honored One, you have taught about quietude and vision
supported by the doctrine [of the great vehicle] and not supported
by [that] doctrine. What do these terms mean?"

The Buddha answered the Bodhisattva Maitreya and said:
"Good son, the quietude and vision supported by the doctrine are
that quietude and vision attained through the doctrine and its
meaning first received and pondered by the bodhisattvas. The
quietude and vision not supported by the [bodhisattva] doctrine
are the quietude and vision attained not through the images of
the doctrine the bodhisattvas have received and pondered, but
through the instructions and meanings of other teachings, such
as meditation upon decaying and rotting [bodies] or upon the impermanence of all things, the suffering of all conditioned states
of being, the no-self of all things, or the final quiescence of cessation.[32] Such quietude and vision I designate as not supported by
doctrine. But, if they have attained a quietude and vision supported by the [bodhisattva] doctrine, those bodhisattvas I have

designated as followers of the doctrine, and they have keen faculties, while, if they attain a quietude and vision not supported by
doctrine, those bodhisattvas I have designated as followers of faith,
and they have dull faculties."

The Bodhisattva Maitreya addressed the Buddha and said:
"World-honored One, you have taught about quietude and vision
that take as their object different doctrines, and about quietude
and vision that take as their object a unified doctrine. What do
these terms mean?"

The Buddha answered the Bodhisattva Maitreya and said:
"Good son, when a bodhisattva takes as his object of understand-
699a   ing each point of the doctrine of the scriptures, etc., and practices
quietude and vision in regard to these doctrines which he has received and pondered, that is termed quietude and vision that take
as their object different doctrines. When a bodhisattva takes as
the object of his understanding the doctrine of all the scriptures,
etc., and attentively reflects upon all these doctrines as one lump,
one accumulation, one whole, one gathering up, all in harmony
with suchness, turning toward suchness, approaching suchness,
in harmony with wisdom, with cessation, with the conversion of
the support, going toward these; if, in approaching these doctrines
he proclaims the unlimited, incalculable doctrine and with this
reflection practices quietude and vision, that is termed quietude
and vision that take as their object a unified doctrine."

The Bodhisattva Maitreya addressed the Buddha and said:
"World-honored One, you have taught about quietude and vision
that take as their object a minor unified doctrine, about quietude
and vision that take as their object a great unified doctrine, and
about quietude and vision that take as their object an unlimited
unified doctrine. What do these terms mean?"

The Buddha answered the Bodhisattva Maitreya and said:
"Good son, if one takes as the object of understanding the meaning of each of the scriptures and of the other eleven divisions of
the teachings, and attentively reflects upon them as one lump,
etc., this is to be known as the quietude and vision that take as

their object a minor unified doctrine. But if one takes as the object of understanding the doctrine of the scriptures, etc., received and pondered, and attentively reflects upon them as one lump, etc., without considering them separately, then this is to be known as the quietude and vision that take as their object a great unified doctrine. If one takes as the objects of understanding the unlimited doctrinal teaching of the Tathāgata, the unlimited words and expressions of that doctrine, and the unlimited clarifications of ever more excellent wisdom, and attentively reflects upon them as one lump, etc., without considering them separately, then that is to be termed the quietude and vision that take as their object an unlimited unified doctrine."

The Bodhisattva Maitreya addressed the Buddha and said: "World-honored One, why do you say that the bodhisattvas attain quietude and vision that take as their object of understanding the unified doctrine?"

The Buddha answered the Bodhisattva Maitreya and said: "Good son, there are five reasons that should be understood. The first is that when they reflect, from moment to moment they purge away support for all weakness. The second is that they sever all varieties of concepts and take their joy in doctrine. The third is that they understand the unlimited light of doctrine which has no differentiating marks anywhere. The fourth is that they bring forth purified, nonreflective images for the accomplishment of duty. The fifth is that, in order to bring the Dharma body to fulfillment, they encompass that preeminent, wondrous cause for ever-increasing development."

The Bodhisattva Maitreya addressed the Buddha and said: 699b "World-honored One, when are this quietude and vision that take as their object the unified doctrine said to be understood? At what point are they attained?"

The Buddha answered the Bodhisattva Maitreya and said: "Good son, they are said to be understood from the very first stage of utmost joy, and are said to be attained from the third stage of expanding light. Good son, bodhisattvas just beginning their practices should also study and focus upon [these states of quietude and vision] without remiss, even though they are yet unable to be praised [for attaining them]."

The Bodhisattva Maitreya addressed the Buddha and said: "World-honored One, when is it that this quietude and vision are said to be a concentration having both inquiry and judgment? To be a concentration having no inquiry but only judgment? To be a concentration having neither inquiry nor judgment?"

The Buddha answered the Bodhisattva Maitreya and said: "Good son, that quietude and vision are termed a concentration with both investigation and inquiry when they experience and realize doctrinal descriptions as received, investigated, and inquired about, even though they be grossly obvious. That quietude and vision are said to be a concentration having no investigation but only inquiry when they experience and realize doctrinal descriptions as remembered in their subtle light, even though not experiencing or realizing what is grossly obvious. Quietude and vision are said to be a concentration with neither investigation nor inquiry when they experience and realize those doctrinal descriptions without any effort to reflect at all. Furthermore, good son, quietude and vision accompanied by investigation is termed a concentration with both investigation and inquiry. Quietude and vision accompanied by inquiry are termed a concentration that has no investigation but only inquiry. Quietude and vision that take as the content of understanding the unified doctrine are termed a concentration that has neither investigation nor inquiry."

The Bodhisattva Maitreya addressed the Buddha and said: "World-honored One, what are the marks of quietude? What are the marks of the initiative [for vision]? What are the marks of abandonment?"

The Buddha answered the Bodhisattva Maitreya and said: "Good son, whenever thinking becomes flighty or is about to become flighty, quietude is characterized as a focusing upon those things that can engender disgust, or by a focusing upon thinking uninterrupted [by images]. Whenever thinking becomes languid or is about to become languid, initiative [for vision] is characterized as a focusing upon those things that can bring joy, or by a focusing upon the images of that thinking. Whenever one becomes defiled by these two passionate inclinations, whether in the practice of quietude, the practice of vision, or the practice of both in synergy, abandonment is characterized as an effortless focusing and spontaneity of mind."

The Bodhisattva Maitreya addressed the Buddha and said: "World-honored One, that entire multitude of those bodhisattvas who practice quietude and vision know both doctrine and its meaning. What is knowing doctrine? What is knowing its meaning?" 699c

The Buddha answered the Bodhisattva Maitreya and said: "Good son, all those bodhisattvas understand and know doctrine in five aspects, for they know its names, its phrases, its descriptions, its differences, and its unity. The knowledge of its names consists in [knowing its] conceptual designations, which delineate essences in all defiled and purified things. The knowing of its phrases consists in the ability to maintain and establish in discourse all defiled and purified things among that collection of names. The knowing of its writings consists in [knowing] the words that are based upon these two supports [of names and phrases]. The knowing of its differences consists in focusing, which objectifies each of those differences. The knowing of its unity consists in focusing, which objectifies that unity. When all of these come together into one, that is knowing doctrine. This is why it is said that those bodhisattvas know doctrine.

"Good son, those bodhisattvas know meaning in ten aspects, for they know the limit of being, the suchness of being, the meaning of subject, the meaning of object, the meaning of environment, the meaning of enjoyment, the meaning of mistakes, the meaning of the absence of mistakes, the meaning of defilement, and the meaning of purification.

"Good son, the limit of being refers to the limit to the analysis of all that exists among all defiled and purified things. This includes all that exists, such as the five aggregates, the six bases of internal consciousness, and the six bases of external consciousness.

"The suchness of all things refers to suchness existing in all defiled and purified things. This term includes the suchness of all things. There are seven kinds. The first is the suchness of the transmigratory flow, for all conditioned states of being have neither beginning nor end. The second is the suchness of descriptive marks, for in all things both persons and things have no-self. The third is the suchness of conscious construction, for all conditioned states of being are nothing but conscious construction. The fourth is the suchness of what is given, that is, the truth about suffering that I have preached. The fifth is the suchness of false conduct, that is, the truth about the origin [of suffering] that I have preached. The sixth is the suchness of purification, that is, the truth of the destruction [of suffering] that I have preached. And the seventh is the suchness of correct practice, that is, the truth of the path that I have preached.

"Understand that because of the suchness of the transmigratory flow, of the suchness of what has been given, and the suchness of false conduct, all sentient beings are entirely equal. Because of the suchness of descriptive marks and the suchness of conscious construction, all things are entirely equal. Because of the suchness of purification, the supreme awakenings of all word-hearers, all solitary enlightened ones, and all bodhisattvas are entirely equal. Because of the suchness of correct practice, the wisdoms encompassed in the hearing of doctrine and in the quietude and vision that take as their object the unified realm of doctrine are entirely equal.

700a

"The meaning of subject consists in the five sense organs, mind, thought, sense consciousness, and concomitant mental states.

"The meaning of object consists in the six external bases, for the meaning of subject is also the meaning of object [since the object is nothing but conscious construction].

"The meaning of environment consists in that encompassing environment within which all sentient beings dwell, whether a single town, a hundred towns, a thousand towns, or a hundred thousand towns; whether a single great land bordering the ocean, a hundred such, a thousand such, or a hundred thousand such; whether a single continent of Jambudvīpa, a hundred such, a thousand such, or a hundred thousand such; whether a single group of four continents, a hundred such, a thousand such, or a hundred thousand such; whether a single chiliomicrocosmos, a hundred such, a thousand such, or a hundred thousand such; whether a large dichiliomedzocosmos, a hundred such, a thousand such, or a hundred thousand such; whether a trichiliomegacosmos, a hundred such, a thousand such, a hundred thousand such, or a hundred hundred thousand such, a single billion such, a hundred billion such, a thousand billion such, or a hundred thousand billion such; whether a single trillion, a hundred trillion such, a thousand trillion such, or a hundred thousand trillion such, in number equal to the minute atoms contained in a hundred thousand trillion trichiliomegacosmos, in the unlimited and incalculable encompassing universes in the ten directions.

"The meaning of enjoyment consists in bringing together the requisites I have taught so that sentient beings may come to enjoyment.

"The meaning of mistakes consists in errors of conceptualizing; errors of thinking; errors of seeing in regard to the meaning of subjectivity and objectivity, such as imagining what is impermanent to be eternal; errors of conceptualizing; errors of thinking; and errors of seeing, such as imagining suffering to be happiness or defilement to be purity, or imagining the no-self to be a self.

"The meaning of the absence of mistakes consists in the opposite of the above, whereby one is able to counteract [mistakes]. One must, however, know their marks [to do so].

"The meaning of defilement is triple, for there are three kinds of defilement in this triple world: the defilement of passion, the defilement of our actions, and the defilement of birth.

"The meaning of purification consists in the factors of awakening, whereby one is separated from bondage to those three kinds of defilement.

"These ten aspects encompass all meaning. Moreover, good son, those bodhisattvas are said to know meaning because they are able to know and understand five kinds of meaning, for they know all matters, all meanings, and all causes, they attain the results of perfect knowing, and they understand them.

"Good son, herein the knowing of all matters consists in knowing all that is knowable: i.e., all aggregates, all internal bases, and all external bases. In like fashion the universal knowing of all meaning consists in knowing the meanings that must be distinguished as to their varieties; whether conventional meaning or ultimate meaning; whether virtuous or defective; whether about conditions or times; whether about arising, abiding, or passing away; whether about sickness, etc.; whether about suffering, its origin, etc.; whether about suchness, the reality limit, the reality realm, etc.; whether extensive or specific; whether categorical, analytic, oppositional, or dismissive; whether underlying or explicit. The knowing of all such varieties is what is termed knowing all meaning. The knowing of all causes consists in the factors of awakening, which are able to comprehend both of the preceding [meanings of all matters and all meanings], that is, the stations of recollection, true severance, etc. The attainment of the result of perfect knowing consists in eternal severance from covetousness, anger, and delusion: i.e., discipline and complete severance from covetousness, anger, and delusion; the results [attained] by monks; and the common and exclusive, worldly or transcendent good qualities of word-hearers or Tathāgatas, all of which I have explained. The communication of them, i.e., the communication of the things [above], consists in broadly proclaiming and announcing to others all those liberating wisdoms of the doctrine that one has realized. These five meanings encompass all meaning.

"Moreover, good son, those bodhisattvas are said to know meaning because they know the four aspects of meaning: the meaning of the appropriation of thinking, the meaning of experience, the meaning of conscious construction, and the meaning of defilement and purification. Good son, these four aspects of meaning encompass all meaning.

"Moreover, good son, those bodhisattvas are said to know meaning because they know the three aspects of meaning: the meaning of expressions, the meaning of meaning, and the meaning of realms. Good son, the meaning of expressions refers to the collection of words, etc. The meaning of meaning is of ten kinds: the marks of reality, the marks of universal knowing, the marks of final severance, the marks of realization, the marks of cultivation, the marks of the differences between reality and the other [four items above], the marks of the synergy between support and supported, the marks of the obstacles to universal knowing, the marks of the states harmonious with that [universal knowing], and the marks of the wretchedness of the absence of universal knowing and the advantage of its presence. The meaning of realms is fivefold: the realm of the surrounding world, the realm of sentient beings, the realm of doctrine, the realm of discipline, and the realm of the methods of discipline. Good son, these three aspects encompass all meaning."

The Bodhisattva Maitreya addressed the Buddha and said: "World-honored One, what is the difference between meaning known through wisdom gained from hearing [doctrine], meaning known through wisdom gained from thinking, and meaning known through wisdom gained from the cultivation of quietude and vision?"

The Buddha answered the Bodhisattva Maitreya and said: "Good son, [in the case of] the wisdom gained from hearing [doctrine], [bodhisattvas] rely upon the literal meaning of a text without really understanding its intent or making it clear. They move toward liberation without being able to realize the meaning that brings about that liberation. [In the case of] the wisdom gained from thinking, [bodhisattvas] also rely upon the text, but not just to the letter, for they are able really to understand its intent. But they are not yet able to make [that intent] clear, and, although they turn toward liberation, they are yet unable to realize the meaning that brings about that liberation. [In the case of] the

700c

wisdom gained from cultivation, bodhisattvas both rely upon the text and do not rely upon the text, they both follow the letter and do not follow the letter, for they are able really to understand its intent. They make [that intent] clear by means of images wrought in concentration that conform to the matters to be known. They turn toward liberation well and are able to realize the meaning that brings that liberation about. Good son, these are what are termed the three kinds of differences in knowing meaning."

The Bodhisattva Maitreya addressed the Buddha and said: "World-honored One, what is the wisdom and what is the insight of all those bodhisattvas who know doctrine and its meaning through their cultivation of quietude and vision?"

The Buddha answered the Bodhisattva Maitreya and said: "Good son, I have already on numerous occasions proclaimed the two differences between wisdom and insight! Nevertheless, I will now summarize the main point for you. Wisdom is that wondrous discernment which occurs through the cultivation of that quietude and vision which take as their object the unified doctrine [of the great vehicle]. Insight is that wondrous discernment which occurs through the cultivation of that quietude and vision which take as their object the different doctrines [of the great vehicle]."

The Bodhisattva Maitreya addressed the Buddha and said: "World-honored One, when the bodhisattvas cultivate quietude and vision, what images do they abandon? By means of what reflections?"

The Buddha answered the Bodhisattva Maitreya and said: "Good son, because they reflect upon true suchness, they abandon images of doctrine and images of meaning. When they lack anything to be attained in names and name-essences, then they no longer pay any regard to the images that support those [names and name-essences]. In such a fashion they abandon them. As it is with names, so it is with phrases and all kinds of meanings. Even in regard to realms and essences of realms they lack anything to be attained, and so they no longer pay any regard to their images. In such a fashion they abandon them."

"World-honored One, the meaning of suchness thus discerned [in that reflection] is a meaning [carried by] an image. Is this image of true suchness also to be abandoned or not?"

"Good son, in the meaning of true suchness which they discern, there is no image whatsoever and nothing to be attained. How then could it be abandoned? Good son, as I have explained it, that meaning of true suchness which they discern dispenses with any kind of image that might [carry] any meaning. Thus it is not the case that this discernment itself can be replaced with anything else."

"World-honored One, you have given the examples of the broken water basin, the dirty mirror, and the bubbling spring as being surfaces that do not sustain any surface image for consideration. The opposite of these would then sustain [that image]. In like fashion, if one has a mind not cultivated, then one will not sustain a true understanding of suchness, but when that mind is well cultivated, then one will sustain such an understanding. In this explanation, what is the thinking that is capable of such a penetrating understanding? What kind of suchness were you talking about?"

701a

"Good son," [the Buddha answered,] "in that explanation there are three kinds of thinking capable of penetrating understanding: the thinking that is capable of understanding from what has been heard, the thinking that is capable of understanding from what has been thought, and the thinking that is capable of understanding from what has been cultivated. I presented that explanation in light of the suchness of conscious construction."

"World-honored One, those bodhisattvas have discerned and know both doctrine and meanings and have been earnest in their cultivation to abandon all images. How many kinds of difficult-to-abandon images do they abandon? And how do they in fact abandon them?"

"Good son, there are ten kinds of such images, and those bodhisattvas are able to abandon them through emptiness. First, because they discern and know both doctrine and meanings, there are the various images of writings and words, which they are able to abandon through [cultivating meditation on] the emptiness of all doctrine. Second, because they discern and know the meaning of the suchness of the given, they have images of arising, passing away, abiding, differentiation, continuity, and development, which they are able to abandon through [cultivating meditation on] first the emptiness of images, and then the emptiness of beginnings and endings. Third, because they discern and know the meaning of the subject, they have lustful images of bodies and of self-pride, which they are able to abandon through [cultivating meditation on] the emptiness of interior [states] and the emptiness of nonattainment. Fourth, because they discern and know the meaning of object, they have images of desired possessions, which they are able to abandon through [cultivating meditation on] the emptiness of externals. Fifth, because they discern and know the meaning of enjoyment, they have internally established images of the flirtations and endowments of men and women, which they are able to abandon through [cultivating meditation on] the emptiness of the internal and the external, and on original emptiness. Sixth, because they discern and know the meaning of environment, they have unlimited images, which they are able to abandon through [cultivating meditation on] the greatness of emptiness. Seventh, because they discern and know the immaterial, they have images of internal quiescence and liberation, which they are able to abandon through [cultivating meditation on] the emptiness of the conditioned. Eighth, because they discern and know the meaning of the true suchness of images, they have images of the no-self of persons and things, which, whether images of only conscious construction or of ultimate meaning, they are able to abandon through [cultivating meditation on] the emptiness of the ultimate, the emptiness of no-essence, the emptiness of the essence of no-essence, and the emptiness of ultimate meaning. Ninth, because they discern and know the meaning of the suchness of purification, they have images of the unconditioned and of the unchanging, which they are able to abandon through [cultivating meditation on] the emptiness of the unconditioned and the emptiness of the unchanging. Tenth, because they attentively reflect upon the nature of emptiness whereby they discipline what has to be disciplined, they have images of the nature of emptiness, which they are able to abandon through [cultivating meditation on] the emptiness of emptiness."

"World-honored One, once they have abandoned these ten kinds of images, what other images do they abandon and from what images are they liberated?"

701b

"Good son, they abandon the images wrought in concentration. They are liberated from and abandon the binding images of defilement. Good son, you should understand that, strictly speaking, each of these emptinesses counteracts its respective images, but yet it is not true that each one does not counteract all the images. It is similar to the case of ignorance, for it is not true that it is unable to engender all the defiled things even up to old age and dying. However, strictly speaking, ignorance is said to engender only karmic formations, because all the karmic formations are immediately caused by ignorance. This same principle also applies [to the emptinesses]."

At that time the Bodhisattva Maitreya addressed the Buddha and said: "World-honored One, what is the overall image of that emptiness which the bodhisattvas discern without discarding and yet without [engendering] pride in regard to that image of emptiness?"

Then the World-honored One praised the Bodhisattva Maitreya and said: "Excellent! Excellent! Good son, you have been able to question the Tathāgata on this profound meaning in order to lead all the bodhisattvas not to discard the image of the nature of emptiness. Why is this so, good son? It is because if the bodhisattvas were to discard the image of the nature of emptiness, then they would discard the great vehicle altogether. Therefore attend well, for I will explain the overall image of emptiness for you. Good son, in the great vehicle the overall image of emptiness refers to the final separation of those images clung to by imagination, with all their varieties of defilement and purity, from both

67

the pattern of other-dependency and the pattern of full perfection: [i.e.,] the complete nonattainment [of such imagined things] in those [patterns of consciousness]."

The Bodhisattva Maitreya addressed the Buddha and said: "World-honored One, how many concentrations are included within this quietude and vision?"

The Buddha addressed the Bodhisattva Maitreya and said: "Good son, as I have explained, the unlimited word-hearers, bodhisattvas, and Tathāgatas have unlimited varieties of concentration, all of which are included within [quietude and vision]."

"World-honored One, what is the cause of this quietude and vision?"

"Good son, it is purified discipline and true insight accomplished through purified hearing and reflection."

"World-honored One, what are the results of this quietude and vision?"

"Good son, their results are well-purified discipline, well-purified thought, and well-purified understanding. Moreover, good son, all the good qualities, both worldly and transcendent, of all word-hearers, Tathāgatas, etc., are included as results of this quietude and vision."

"World-honored One, what activity is performed through this quietude and vision?"

"Good son, their activity is the liberation from the two bonds, the bonds of images and the bonds of gross weakness."

"World-honored One, among the five kinds of entanglements you have explained, which are obstacles to quietude, which to vision, and which to both together?"

"Good son, lust for bodies and possessions is the obstacle to quietude. Lack of interest in the holy doctrines is the obstacle to knowledge. The various ways of abiding in the welter of pleasurable images and being fully content with shallowness are the obstacles to both together. Because of the first [entanglement], one is unable to perform meditation. Because of the second, the effort cultivated never reaches accomplishment."

"World-honored One, among the five obfuscations, which impede quietude, which vision, and which both together?"

"Good son, flightiness and evildoing are obstacles to quietude. Melancholy, laziness, and doubt are obstacles to vision. Covetousness and annoyance are obstacles to both together."

"World-honored One, how does one determine the degree to which the path of quietude has been perfected and purified?"

"Good son, to the degree that melancholy and laziness have been eradicated, to that degree one says that the path of quietude has been perfected and purified."

"World-honored One, how does one determine the degree to which the path of vision has been perfected and purified?"

"Good son, to the degree that flightiness and evil actions have been eradicated, to that degree one says that the path of vision has been perfected and purified."

"World-honored One, in realizing quietude and vision, of how many distractions must bodhisattvas be aware?"

"Good son, they must be aware of five: distraction in regard to [their] attention, distraction in regard to externals, distraction in regard to internals, distraction in regard to images, and the distraction of gross weakness. Good son, if bodhisattvas reject attending to the great vehicle and fall into the attending of word-hearers and solitary enlightened ones, that is distraction in regard to [their] attending. If they allow their minds to be scattered among the passionate inclinations perceived upon all the confusing images of the five external sense attractions, that is distraction in regard to externals. If they become immersed in melancholy, attached to the taste of trance through laziness, or defiled by the accompanying passion for any other trance state, that is the distraction in regard to internals. If, in attending to and thinking upon the images wrought by means of interior concentration, they rely upon images of external things, that is the distraction in regard to images. If internally they attend to sensations that arise conditionally and yet, because of their gross weakness, imagine a self and engender pride, that is the distraction of gross weakness."

"World-honored One, what are the obstacles that this quietude and vision are capable of counteracting from the initial bodhisattva stage to the Tathāgata stage?"

"Good son, in the first stage they counteract the obstacles of the passions that lead to evil destinies, and of the defilement of action and birth. In the second stage they counteract the obstacle of the appearance of subtle sins. In the third stage they counteract the obstacle of the desires. In the fourth stage they counteract the obstacle of attachment to concentration and to doctrine. In the fifth stage they counteract the obstacle of rejecting transmigration altogether and going [directly] to cessation. In the sixth stage they counteract the obstacle of the frequent appearing of images. In the seventh stage they counteract the obstacle of the appearing of subtle images. In the eighth stage they counteract the obstacles of expending effort in regard to the imageless and of not having attained mastery in regard to images. In the ninth stage they counteract the obstacle of not having attained mastery of all the varieties of skillful speech. In the tenth stage they counteract the obstacle of not having attained the realization of the fully perfected Dharma body. Good son, in the Tathāgata stage this quietude and vision counteract both the obstacle of the most subtle passion and the obstacle to the knowable. Because they are thus able to completely eradicate these obstacles, they finally realize universal wisdom and insight, unattached and unhindered; and, supported upon the accomplishment of [their] objective, they are installed in the ultimately pure Dharma body."

The Bodhisattva Maitreya addressed the Buddha and said: "World-honored One, how do bodhisattvas, supported upon their intense cultivation of quietude and vision, realize supreme awakening?"

The Buddha answered the Bodhisattva Maitreya and said: "Good son, having already attained quietude and vision, the bodhisattvas support themselves upon the seven suchnesses. With minds well concentrated upon the doctrine [they have] heard and pondered, within themselves they truly reflect upon the nature of suchness as it has been well considered, well examined, and well established. Because of their reflection upon suchness, they are able to abandon the appearances of all subtle images, not to mention gross images. Good son, these subtle images refer to images of the appropriation of thinking; images of experience; images of conscious construction; images of defilement and purification; images of the interior; images of the exterior; images of both interior and exterior; images that one must act for the benefit of sentient beings; images of true wisdom; images of suchness, images of [the four truths of] suffering, its origin, its destruction, and the path; images of the conditioned; images of the unconditioned; images of eternity; images of transience; images of the nature of suffering and change; images of the unchanging; images of the different characteristics of the conditioned; images of the identical characteristics of the conditioned; the image that there is a universal just because one knows a universal; images of the no-self of persons; and images of the no-self of things.

"They are able to abandon all thoughts that appear in their 702b minds and, because they continually abide in such an activity, over a period of time they cultivate a mind to counteract all entanglements, obfuscations, and distractions. Afterwards, they internally engender penetrating discernment in regard to each of the seven suchnesses, for this is the path of insight. Because of this attainment they are said to have entered the assured status of a bodhisattva exempt from rebirth, for they are born into the household of the Tathāgata and, entering into the first stage, they are able to enjoy the superior good qualities of this stage. During this initial period, because they have attained quietude and vision, they have already attained the two objects—the objects accompanied by images for reflection and the objects that are not accompanied by images for reflection—for it is at this point that they attain the path of insight. They also realize as the object of their understanding the limits of the phenomenal. Then afterwards in all the stages they cultivate the path of meditation while attentively reflecting upon these three kinds of objects. Just like a man who removes a large wedge by means of a small wedge, so these bodhisattvas banish internal images by the method of relying upon this [meditation] as the small wedge to remove the large wedge [of all their images]. All images that pertain to defilement are abolished, and, being so abolished, weakness is also abolished. Since they destroy forever that weakness in all its images, afterwards in all the stages they gradually refine their thoughts as one refines gold until they realize supreme awakening, until they realize the objective they set out to accomplish. Good son, thus because these bodhisattvas have well cultivated meditation within themselves, they realize supreme awakening."

The Bodhisattva Maitreya addressed the Buddha and said: "World-honored One, how does this cultivation [of meditation] produce the great majesty of a bodhisattva?"

"Good son, when the bodhisattvas become aware of the six supports, they are able to produce that great majesty of a bodhisattva. The first is that they know well the arising of thought. The second is that they know well the abiding of thought. The third is that they know well the departure of thought. The fourth is that they know well the increasing of thought. The fifth is that they know well the diminution of thought. The sixth is that they know well the methods. They know well the arising of thought, for they truly know the differences that engender thought in its sixteen activities, and this is what is meant by knowing well the arising of thought.

"These sixteen activities of thought are as follows. The first is the arising of conscious construction as the unconscious, foundational receptacle, that is, the appropriating consciousness. The second is the arising of conscious construction in tandem with its numerous different objects, that is, the imaginative thought consciousness that immediately apprehends all the object realms of material forms, etc.; the understanding which immediately apprehends internal and external objects; or, alternately, the imaginative thought consciousness which in an instant, a single moment, enters into concentration and sees many Buddha lands and many

Tathāgatas. The third is the arising of conscious construction
objectified in small images, that is, thinking bound to the world of
desire. The fourth is the arising of conscious construction objectified
in large images, that is, thinking bound to the world of material
form. The fifth is the arising of conscious construction objectified
in unlimited images, that is, thinking bound to infinite space and
infinite consciousness. The sixth is the arising of conscious construction objectified in subtle images, that is, thinking bound neither to conceptualization nor to nonconceptualization. The eighth
is the arising of conscious construction in no images, that is, transcendent thinking and objectless thinking. The ninth is the arising of conscious construction activated in tandem with suffering,
that is, the thinking of the inhabitants of the hells. The tenth is
the arising of conscious construction in tandem with the complex
of sensation, that is, thinking activated through desire. The eleventh is the arising of conscious construction activated in tandem
with joy, that is, the thinking of the first two meditations. The
twelfth is the arising of conscious construction activated in tandem with happiness, that is, the thinking of the third meditation.
The thirteenth is the arising of conscious construction activated
in tandem with neither suffering nor happiness, that is, thinking
from the fourth meditation to neither conceptualization nor
nonconceptualization. The fourteenth is the arising of conscious
construction in tandem with defilement, that is, the thinking
associated with passions and passionate inclinations. The
fifteenth is the arising of conscious construction in tandem with
goodness, that is, thinking associated with faith, etc. The six-
teenth is the arising of conscious construction in tandem with
morally neutral states, that is, thinking unassociated with either
that [faith or that passion].

"How do they know well the abiding of thought? This means
that they truly know the suchness of understanding. How do they
know well the departure of thought? This means that they truly
know deliverance from the two bonds, those of images and those of
weakness, for such knowing enables them to lead their thinking

away from them. How do they know well the increase of thought? When they truly know the thoughts that are able to counteract the bonds of images and the bonds of weakness, for at the moment when those [images and weaknesses] increase and accumulate, they attain an increase and accumulation [of countering thoughts]. This is what is meant by knowing the increase of thought. How do they know well the decrease of thought? They truly know the images that have to be counteracted, the weak, defiled thoughts, and, when they discard them or lessen them, this is a rejecting and a decreasing. This is what is meant by knowing the decrease of thought. How do they know well methods? They truly know the liberations, the [realms] of mastery, and [the realms of] totality, either when cultivating [them] or terminating [that cultivation]. Good son, this is how the bodhisattvas [produce] the great majesty of a bodhisattva, whether they have already done so, are going to do so, or are presently doing so."

The Bodhisattva Maitreya addressed the Buddha and said: "World-honored One, as you have taught, in cessation without remainder all sensations without remainder are forever destroyed. Which are these sensations that are forever destroyed?"

"Good son, in sum, there are two kinds of sensations destroyed without remainder. The first are the sensations of bodily weakness, while the second are the sensations of the objects that are their results. There are four kinds of sensations of bodily weakness: the sensations of bodies of material form, the sensations of formless bodies, the sensations of weakness already brought to term as result, and the sensations of weakness not yet brought to term as result. Sensations already brought to term as result refer to present sensations, while sensations not yet brought to term as result refer to the objects of sensation to be caused in the future [by those present sensations]. Sensations of objects that result [from the sensations of bodily weakness] are also of four kinds: sensations of place, sensations of requisites, sensations of enjoyment, and sensations of romantic leanings. In cessation with remainder, all sensations not yet brought to term as result have

703a

already been destroyed, for there is generally present the experiencing of sensations born from wisdom contact, which counteract the experiencing both of those [sensations not yet brought to term as result], and of those sensations already brought to term as result. Those two kinds of sensation are already destroyed, and one experiences only that sensation born of wisdom contact. But in cessation without remainder, at the time of final cessation even this [kind of wisdom sensation] is eternally destroyed. Thus it is said that in the realm of cessation without remainder, all sensations are destroyed without remainder." Thus the World-honored One finished his explanation.

He again addressed the Bodhisattva Maitreya and said: "Excellent, excellent, good son, that you have been able to question the Tathāgata about the accomplishment of the most pure path of wondrous centering. You yourself have already certainly attained utmost skill, and I already have proclaimed for you the path of wondrous centering, perfect and most pure. The awakened ones of the past or the future have already taught or will teach a like teaching. All good sons and good daughters must with diligent effort cultivate it."

Then the World-honored One recited verses to emphasize his meaning:

> If one acts in an unrestrained manner in regard to centering as presented in this doctrine, one will lose its great benefit. But if, relying upon this doctrine and centering, one correctly cultivates and practices it, one will attain the great awakening. If, looking to what they can attain, some reject and criticize [this doctrine] and take their view to be the way to realize doctrine, Maitreya, they will be as far from centering as is the sky from the earth. Obdurate people who do not work to benefit beings, once enlightened, do not bother about benefiting sentient beings, but the wise do act [for others] until the end of the eons, and they attain supreme, undefiled joy. If one enunciates doctrine from

desire, although one be said to have rejected desire, one will revert to desire. Thus fools, having attained the priceless doctrine, turn back and wander about begging alms. Rejecting contentious quarreling and abandoning attachment to opinion, engender superior effort. In order to deliver gods and men, you must study this centering.

At that time the Bodhisattva Maitreya addressed the Buddha and said: "World-honored One, how should we designate this teaching in this doctrinal discourse on explicating underlying intent? How should we revere it?"

703b The Buddha answered the Bodhisattva Maitreya and said: "Good son, it is designated the teaching on the explicit meaning of centering and you should revere it as such." When this teaching on the explicit meaning of centering was preached in the assembly, six hundred thousand sentient beings attained supreme awakening; three hundred thousand word-hearers attained purification of their doctrine-eye, undefiled and unpolluted in regard to this doctrine; one hundred fifty thousand word-hearers exhausted their contaminants and their thought attained liberation; and seventy-five thousand bodhisattvas came to attend to expansive centering.[33]

Chapter VII

The Stages and Perfections

At that time the Bodhisattva Avalokiteśvara addressed the Buddha and said: "World-honored One, you have taught the bodhisattva stages, which are the stage of utmost joy, the stage of purification, the stage of expanding light, the stage of flaming wisdom, the stage of invincibility, the stage of presence, the stage far-reaching, the stage unshakable, the stage of wisdom discernment, and the stage of the doctrine cloud. You have furthermore described the Buddha stage as an eleventh stage. What are the purifications of these stages? In what [stages] are [those purifications] included?"

At that time the Buddha addressed the Bodhisattva Avalokiteśvara and said: "Good son, you should understand that all these stages are included in the four purifications and the eleven aspects. The four purifications are able to encompass the ten stages because the purification of superior intention encompasses the first stage, the purification of superior discipline encompasses the second stage, the purification of superior thought encompasses the third stage, and the purification of superior wisdom encompasses the excellences evolved in the subsequent stages. You should understand that [this purification] is able to encompass all the stages from the fourth to the last Buddha stage. You should understand that in this fashion these four purifications are able to encompass all the stages.

"How do the eleven aspects encompass all these stages? In the first stage of practicing commitment, the bodhisattvas well cultivate patience in their commitment by relying upon the ten practices [of copying, honoring, propagating, attending to, reading, maintaining, explaining, intoning, pondering, and cultivating] doctrine. Therefore, upon transcending this stage, they enter the assured status of a bodhisattva exempt from rebirth. Having thus brought this [first] aspect to perfection, those bodhisattvas are yet unable truly to know and practice, because of the presence of subtle sins

703c and mistakes. Therefore, in this aspect they are yet imperfect. But they are able to realize this perfection by the earnest cultivation [of meditation]. Having thus perfected this [second] aspect, they are yet unable to attain a worldly perfect concentration or recollection, or a perfect memory of [doctrine] they have heard. Therefore, in this aspect they are yet imperfect. But they are able to realize this perfection by the earnest cultivation [of meditation]. Having thus perfected this [third] aspect, they are yet unable to hold the factors of wisdom they have attained in prolonged meditation. Their minds are yet incapable of abandoning attachment to recollection and doctrine. Therefore, in this aspect they are yet imperfect. But they are able to realize this perfection through the earnest cultivation [of meditation]. Having thus perfected this [fourth] aspect, they are yet unable to examine the principles of the holy truths as they are in reality. They are unable to turn away from an exclusive rejection of transmigration and an exclusive focusing upon cessation. They are unable to cultivate the factors of wisdom comprised in skillful methods. Therefore in this aspect they are yet imperfect. But they are able to realize this perfection through their earnest cultivation [of meditation]. Having thus perfected this [fifth] aspect, they are yet unable to examine the evolution of transmigration as it is in reality, because they frequently engender disgust for that [transmigration]. They are unable to abide for long in imageless reflection [on transmigration]. Therefore, in this aspect they are yet imperfect. But they are able to realize this perfection through the earnest cultivation [of meditation]. Having thus perfected this [sixth] aspect, they are yet unable to abide for long in the meditation of imageless reflection in a nondefective and uninterrupted fashion.

Therefore, in this aspect they are yet imperfect. But they are able 704a to realize this perfection through the earnest cultivation [of meditation]. Having thus perfected this [seventh] aspect, they are yet unable to abandon effort in regard to imageless mastery. They are unable to attain mastery over images. Therefore, in this aspect they are yet imperfect. But they are able to realize this perfection through the earnest cultivation [of meditation]. Having thus perfected this [eighth] aspect, they are yet unable to attain mastery over different ways of saying things, images, interpretations, and distinctions in their preaching. Therefore, in this aspect they are yet imperfect. But they are able to realize this perfection through the earnest cultivation [of meditation]. Having thus perfected this [ninth] aspect, they are yet unable to attain the sense of the presence of the perfect Dharma body. Therefore, in this aspect they are yet imperfect. But they are able to realize this perfection through the earnest cultivation [of meditation]. Having thus perfected this [tenth] aspect, they are yet unable to attain that wondrous wisdom and insight, unattached and unimpeded in all knowable realms whatsoever. Therefore, in this aspect they are yet imperfect. But they are able to realize this perfection through the earnest cultivation [of meditation]. Thus this aspect is brought to perfection; and, being perfected, all these aspects are brought to perfection. Good son, understand how in this manner these eleven aspects entirely include the ten stages."

The Bodhisattva Avalokiteśvara addressed the Buddha and said: "World-honored One, why is the first stage termed the stage of utmost joy? Why are the other stages termed what they are termed?"

The Buddha answered the Bodhisattva Avalokiteśvara and said: "Good son, the first stage is termed the stage of utmost joy because, in accomplishing great meaning and attaining a transcendent mind not hitherto attained in the world, one engenders great delight and joy. The second stage is termed the stage of purification because in it one removes all subtle transgressions against discipline. The third stage is termed the stage of expanding light because the concentrations and memory formulas attained in it are able to be the support for unlimited wisdom light. The fourth stage is termed the stage of flaming wisdom because the factors of wisdom attained in it burn away all passion and wisdom flares up like fire. The fifth stage is termed the stage of invincibility because when in it, one attains mastery in the cultivation of skillful methods over those same factors of wisdom, which are most difficult to overcome. The sixth stage is termed the stage of presence because when in it, one brings to presence and examines all the evolutions of conditioned states of being and abides in their presence by the continual cultivation of reflection upon the imageless. The seventh stage is termed the far-reaching stage because when in it, one is able to enter into an imageless and far-reaching reflection, without defect and without interruption, and thus one draws near to images of pure lands. The eighth stage is termed the unshakable stage because when in it, one attains spontaneity in regard to the imageless and does not evince any movement of any passion in regard to images. The ninth stage is termed the stage of wisdom discernment because in it one obtains irreproachable and expansive wisdom which understands and masters all doctrinal enunciations. The tenth stage is termed the stage of the doctrine [Dharma] cloud because in it, just as a great cloud is able to cover over the sky, this mass of weakness [i.e., the receptacle consciousness] is encompassed by the Dharma body. The eleventh stage is termed the Buddha stage because in it one is forever

704b freed from the obstacle of even the subtlest passion, and from the obstacle to the knowable, in supreme awakening to all knowable realms."

The Bodhisattva Avalokiteśvara addressed the Buddha and said: "World-honored One, in the [ten] stages, how many delusions and how many weaknesses to be counteracted are found?"

The Buddha answered the Bodhisattva Avalokiteśvara and said: "Good son, in these stages there are twenty-two delusions and twelve kinds of weakness to be counteracted. In the first stage there are two delusions: the delusion of clinging to personality and to things, and the delusion of being defiled in evil destinies. These, together with the weakness [resulting from them], are what has to be counteracted [by this first stage]. In the second stage there are two delusions: the delusion of subtle mistakes and the delusion of destinies [resulting] from various actions. These, together with the weakness that [issues from them], are what are to be counteracted [by this second stage]. In the third stage there are two delusions: the delusion of being covetous [of sense objects] and the delusion in regard to perfecting the memory of what is heard. These, together with the weakness [that issues from them], are what are to be counteracted [by this third stage]. In the fourth stage there are two delusions: the delusion of being attached to concentration and the delusion of being attached to doctrine. These, together with the weakness [that issues from them], are what are to be counteracted [by this fourth stage]. In the fifth stage there are two delusions: the delusion of an exclusive focus in rejecting transmigration and the delusion of an exclusive focus in aiming at cessation. These, together with the weakness [that issues from them], are what are to be counteracted [by this fifth stage]. In the sixth stage there are two delusions: the delusion of bringing to presence and examining the evolutions of conditioned states of being [as defiled], and the delusion in frequently bringing to presence images [as purified]. These, together with the weakness [that issues from them], are what are to be counteracted [by this sixth stage]. In the seventh stage there are two delusions: the delusion of bringing to presence subtle images [of conditioned states] and the delusion [of teaching] by the method of focusing exclusively upon the imageless. These, together with the weakness [that issues from them], are what are to be counteracted [by this seventh stage]. In the eighth stage there are two delusions: the delusion of exerting effort in regard to the imageless and the delusion in regard to mastering images. These, together with the weakness [that issues from them], are what are to be counteracted [by this eighth stage]. In the ninth stage there are two delusions: the delusion that one has mastered the unlimited doctrinal explanations, the

unlimited doctrinal literature, and the successive wisdom interpretations and formulas, and the delusion of having mastered the
art of interpretation. These, together with the weakness [that issues from them], are what are to be counteracted [by this ninth
stage]. In the tenth stage there are two delusions: the delusion in
regard to great clairvoyance and the delusion in discerning subtle
intentions. These, together with the weakness [that issues from
them], are what are to be counteracted [by this tenth stage]. In
the Tathāgata stage there are two delusions: the delusion of a
704c most subtle attachment to all the knowable realms of meaning
and the delusion of their extremely subtle obstacles. These, together with the weakness [that issues from them], are what are to
be counteracted [by this Tathāgata stage]. Good son, it is because
of these twenty-two delusions and eleven weaknesses that there
are these stages, and that supreme awakening, being encumbered
by [the delusions and weaknesses], remains absent."

The Bodhisattva Avalokiteśvara addressed the Buddha and
said: "World-honored One, supreme awakening is rare indeed, for
it is the attainment of the great benefit, the great result, whereby
all bodhisattvas are enabled to break asunder the net of great
delusion, are enabled to pass through the thicket of great weaknesses and realize supreme awakening."

The Bodhisattva Avalokiteśvara addressed the Buddha and
said: "World-honored One, by how many supremacies are these
[ten] stages established?"

The Buddha answered the Bodhisattva Avalokiteśvara and
said: "Good son, in sum there are eight: the purity of high intention, the purity of thought, the purity of compassion, the purity of
perfections, the purity of seeing Buddhas and offering them hom-
age, the purity of maturing sentient beings, the purity of birth,
and the purity of majesty. Good son, these purities in sequence
become increasingly superior from the first stage up to the
Tathāgata stage. Excluding the purity of birth in the Tathāgata
stage, the good qualities of the first stage are equally present in
the higher stages, for you should understand that these stages

are superior in good qualities [to that first stage]. The good qualities of all the ten bodhisattva stages can be surpassed, but the good qualities of the Tathāgata stage are unsurpassed."

The Bodhisattva Avalokiteśvara addressed the Buddha and said: "World-honored One, why do you say that the birth of a bodhisattva is far superior to the births of all other sentient beings?"

The Buddha answered the Bodhisattva Avalokiteśvara and said: "Good son, there are four reasons. First, [that birth] is engendered from the most pure good roots. Second, it is taken up through the power of their penetrating thought. Third, the compassion [of their birth] delivers sentient beings. And fourth, being undefiled, they are able to remove the defilement of others."

The Bodhisattva Avalokiteśvara addressed the Buddha and said: "World-honored One, why do you say that all bodhisattvas produce an expansive vow, a wondrous vow, a superior vow?"

The Buddha answered the Bodhisattva Avalokiteśvara and said: "Good son, there are four reasons. All bodhisattvas are well able to realize the happiness of abiding in cessation. They could quickly realize it, yet they renounce that rapid realization of a joyful abode. Without [being impelled by external] causes or [internal] necessity, they produce the mind of that great vow because they desire to benefit all sentient beings. They remain among great sufferings of various kinds for a prolonged time. Therefore I have said that they produce an expansive vow, a wondrous vow, a superior vow." 705a

The Bodhisattva Avalokiteśvara addressed the Buddha and said: "World-honored One, how many precepts must all the bodhisattvas observe?"

The Buddha answered the Bodhisattva Avalokiteśvara and said: "Good son, the precepts of the bodhisattvas are the six perfections of giving, discipline, patience, zeal, meditation, and wisdom."

The Bodhisattva Avalokiteśvara addressed the Buddha and said: "World-honored One, of these six kinds of precepts, how many are included within the precept of high discipline, how many within the precept of high thinking, and how many within the precept of high wisdom?"

The Buddha answered the Bodhisattva Avalokiteśvara and said: "Good son, the first three are included within the precept of high discipline, the single [perfection of] meditation is included within the precept of high thinking, and [the perfection] of wisdom is included within the precept of high wisdom. I teach that [the perfection] of zeal pervades them all."

The Bodhisattva Avalokiteśvara addressed the Buddha and said: "World-honored One, among these six precepts, how many are included within the requisite of merit and how many are included within the requisite of wisdom?"

The Buddha answered the Bodhisattva Avalokiteśvara and said: "Good son, that which is included within the precept of high discipline is synonymous with that which is included within the requisite of merit. That which is included within the precept of high wisdom is synonymous with that which is included within the requisite of wisdom. I teach that both zeal and meditation pervade both [kinds of requisites]."

The Bodhisattva Avalokiteśvara addressed the Buddha and said: "World-honored One, how do the bodhisattvas observe these six precepts?"

The Buddha answered the Bodhisattva Avalokiteśvara and said: "Good son, there are five aspects under which they must observe these precepts. The first is that from the first they must have an intense faith in the wondrous doctrinal teachings about the perfections as found in the bodhisattva canon. The second is that they must zealously cultivate the wondrous wisdoms accomplished through hearing, reflecting, and meditating in the ten practices concerning doctrine. The third is that they must nurture thoughts of wisdom. The fourth is that they must draw near to a spiritual counselor. The fifth is that they must cultivate good qualities without interruption."

The Bodhisattva Avalokiteśvara addressed the Buddha and said: "World-honored One, why have you presented these precepts as six?"

The Buddha answered the Bodhisattva Avalokiteśvara and said: "Good son, there are two reasons: in order to benefit sentient beings and in order to counteract all the passions, for the first three precepts benefit sentient beings, while the latter three counteract all the passions. The first three benefit sentient beings, for by giving, all bodhisattvas provide requisites to benefit sentient beings. By being disciplined, they benefit sentient beings in sparing them from injury, oppression, and irritation. By their patience under abuse, they are able to benefit sentient beings, enabling them to patiently sustain injury, oppression, and irritation. The latter three counteract all the passions, for by zeal the bodhisattvas, although they may not yet have suppressed all their passions forever or may not yet have eliminated all their passionate inclinations, are able diligently to cultivate good qualities, and all those passions become incapable of reversing their efforts toward goodness. By meditation they do suppress their passions forever, and by wisdom they eliminate their passionate inclinations forever."

705b

The Bodhisattva Avalokiteśvara addressed the Buddha and said: "World-honored One, why have you presented the other perfections as four?"

The Buddha answered the Bodhisattva Avalokiteśvara and said: "Good son, it is because they are aids to the former six perfections. Bodhisattvas, who assist sentient beings by means of the first three perfections [of giving, discipline, and patience], establish [sentient beings] in good by means of taking care of them in the skillful methods of all the [four] kinds of attractions [which are giving to beings, encouraging them with speech, benefiting them with action, and identifying with them]. Therefore, I have taught that the perfection of skillful methods is an aid to the first three perfections.

"But because of bodhisattvas' present condition [in the world], their passions are numerous, and they are yet incapable of uninterrupted practice. Because of their fragile commitment and the worldly quality of their understanding, they are incapable of abiding within their [own] minds. Because they are incapable of properly practicing the exercises heard in the bodhisattva canon, the meditation they do have is unable to produce transcendent discernment. However, they have accumulated the requisite of merit in some small part; and in their minds they do engender a vow to lessen their passions in the future. Because of this vow their passions weaken and they become capable of practicing zeal. Therefore I have taught that the perfection of vow is an aid to the perfection of zeal. When bodhisattvas draw near a spiritual counselor and listen to doctrine with true attention, this becomes a cause for their turning away from an inferior commitment and toward a superior commitment, for they become able to attain an otherworldly understanding. It is this that is termed the perfection of power. Due to such power they become capable of abiding within their [own] minds. Therefore I have preached that the perfection of power aids the perfection of meditation. If such bodhisattvas are able to properly cultivate the exercises they have heard, they become able to produce meditation. And this is what is termed the perfection of wisdom. Because of this wisdom they are able to produce transcendent discernment. Therefore I have preached that the perfection of wisdom is an aid to the perfection of discernment."

705c

The Bodhisattva Avalokiteśvara addressed the Buddha and said: "World-honored One, what is the reason for the sequence of the six perfections in your preaching?"

The Buddha answered the Bodhisattva Avalokiteśvara and said: "Good son, [the former] are the support that enables one to produce the latter. This means that bodhisattvas are able to acquire purified discipline through being generous with their physical possessions [through giving]. They practice patience because they guard discipline. By practicing patience, they become capable of producing zeal. By producing zeal, they become capable of accomplishing meditation. Endowed with meditation, they become able to obtain transcendent discernment. This, then, is the reason for the sequence of the six perfections in my preaching."

The Bodhisattva Avalokiteśvara addressed the Buddha and said: "World-honored One, what are the various subdivisions of these six perfections?"

The Buddha answered the Bodhisattva Avalokiteśvara and said: "Good son, each has three subdivisions. The three subdivisions of giving are the giving of doctrine, the giving of material goods, and the giving of fearlessness. The three subdivisions of discipline are the discipline to turn away from what is not good, the discipline to turn toward what is good, and the discipline to turn toward benefiting sentient beings. The three subdivisions of patience are the patience to endure insult and injury, the patience to abide peacefully in suffering, and the patience to investigate doctrine. The three subdivisions of zeal are the zeal which protects one like armor, the zeal to exert effort in engendering good, and the zeal to exert effort in benefiting sentient beings. The three subdivisions of meditation are the meditation of abiding in happiness, which counteracts all the suffering of passion because it is nondiscriminative, tranquil, very tranquil, and irreproachable; the meditation that engenders the good quality [of concentration]; and the meditation that produces benefit for sentient beings. The three subdivisions of discernment are the discernment that has as its object worldly, conventional truth; the discernment that has as its object the truth of ultimate meaning; and the discernment that has as its object the benefiting of sentient beings."

The Bodhisattva Avalokiteśvara addressed the Buddha and said: "World-honored One, why are these perfections called perfections?"

The Buddha answered the Bodhisattva Avalokiteśvara and said: "Good son, there are five reasons: they are unattached, disinterested, irreproachable, nondiscriminative, and fruitful. They are unattached because they are not attached to the opposites of the perfections. They are disinterested because the thought [that accompanies them] is not bound to the maturation or reward resulting from any of the perfections. They are irreproachable because such perfections have nothing in common with defiled states and are apart from implementing evil methods. They are nondiscriminative because the specific descriptions of these perfections do not cling to their literal meaning. They are fruitful

706a because such perfections, when practiced and accumulated, turn toward and seek the result of supreme awakening."

"World-honored One, what are the opposites of these perfections?"

"Good son, you should understand that there are six such [opposite vices]. The first is looking out for one's own advantage in seeking happiness by hankering after pleasure, wealth, and power. The second is looking out for one's own advantage in indulging the pleasures of body, speech, and mind. The third is looking out for one's own advantage in being impatient when humiliated by others. The fourth is looking out for one's own advantage in not bestirring oneself to practice and in being attached to pleasure. The fifth is looking out for one's own advantage in the hectic confusion and wild activity of the world. The sixth is looking out for one's own advantage in the fabrication of what one sees, hears, understands, knows, and says."

"World-honored One, what is the resultant maturation of all these perfections?"

"Good son, you should understand that in sum there are six kinds. The first is the attainment of great wealth. The second is going to and being born in good destinies. The third is the full joy and happiness of peace and concord. The fourth is being a ruler over sentient beings. The fifth is the absence of bodily torment. The sixth is great renown and fame."

"World-honored One, how do these perfections become mixed up with defiled states?"

"Good son, in sum, there are four such situations: when they are related to the absence of compassion, to the absence of reasonableness, to the absence of continuity, or to the absence of diligence. A situation is unreasonable when, by practicing one perfection, one puts off and neglects the practice of the other perfections."

"World-honored One, what is meant by unskillful methods?"

"Good son, if the bodhisattvas, in benefiting sentient beings through their perfections, were to rely only upon material goods to bring [sentient beings] benefit and render them happy, and would not bother to lead them away from evil or establish them in good, that would be an unskillful method. Why is that, good son? It is because it is not true that the one who does such things is really benefiting sentient beings. Whether one has a small amount or a great heap of excrement and urine, it can never be used as perfume. Similarly, because sentient beings suffer because of their actions, and because their nature is suffering, it is impossible to lead them to happiness simply by the method of providing them with fleeting images of material things. The best benefit would be to establish them in good."

The Bodhisattva Avalokiteśvara addressed the Buddha and said: "World-honored One, how many purifications do all these perfections have?"

The Buddha answered the Bodhisattva Avalokiteśvara and said: "Good son, I have never said that they have purifications other than the five enumerated above [of nonattachment, disinterestedness, irreproachability, nondiscrimination, and fruitfulness]. However, with these [five] as the basis, I will explain the common and specific characteristics of the purifications of these perfections.

"The purifications common to all the perfections number seven. The first is that bodhisattvas need not seek after knowledge other than that of the doctrine. The second is that, after they have gained insight into this doctrine, they do not engender attachment to it. The third is that they do not engender doubt about this doctrine or question whether or not it is capable of leading to great awakening. The fourth is that they never congratulate themselves, deprecate others, or engage in ridicule. The fifth is that they never become prideful or lax. The sixth is that they never denigrate their achievement or become surfeited [with it]. The seventh is that they never become jealous of or stingy with others because of this doctrine.

"The purifications specific to each perfection also number seven. As I have taught, the bodhisattvas are characterized by seven purifications of giving. The first is that, because the gift is pure, they practice a purified giving. The second is that, because their

706b

discipline is pure, they practice a purified giving. The third is that, because their insight is pure, they practice a purified giving. The fourth is that, because their thought is pure, they practice a purified giving. The fifth is that, because their speech is pure, they practice a purified giving. The sixth is that, because their wisdom is pure, they practice a purified giving. The seventh is that, because they are purified from defilement, they practice a purified giving. These are the seven characteristics of the purification of giving.

"Furthermore, all bodhisattvas are able to understand well and observe all the lessons of the code of rules. They are able to understand and separate themselves from what is sinful. They are endowed with enduring discipline. They are endowed with strong discipline. They are endowed with constantly active discipline. They are endowed with constantly prevailing discipline. They accept and learn all lessons. These are the seven characteristics of the purification of discipline.

"Having deep faith in the maturation that results from all their own actions, the bodhisattvas do not become exasperated in any unfavorable situation in which they might find themselves. In order to overcome trouble, they do not become abusive, enraged, pugnacious, threatening, or flippant. They do not harbor resentment or reckon up their due. When criticized, they do not become vexed, but neither do they invite criticism from others. It is not from fear or defiled affection that they practice patience, but they do not spurn kindnesses. These are the seven characteristics of the purification of patience.

"Having understood the equality of zeal, the bodhisattvas neither boast of their resolute practice of zeal nor denigrate others. They are endowed with great power and with great zeal. Their profound abilities are strong and resolute. They never cast off the yoke of the good. These are the seven characteristics of the purification of zeal.

"In their meditation the bodhisattvas have acquired the concentration that penetrates images, the concentration of perfection,

706c

90

the concentration of two aspects, the concentration of spontaneity, the concentration without support, the concentration of inculcating control, and the unlimited concentration of practicing the lessons learned in the bodhisattva canon. These are the seven characteristics of the purification of meditation.

"Discernment means that the bodhisattvas have separated themselves from the two extremes of imposing [imagined essences upon doctrine] or of deleting [conventional meaning from doctrine], for they practice the middle path.[34] Because of this discernment, they truly understand the meaning of liberation methods: that is, the three liberation methods of the empty, the desireless, and the imageless. They truly understand the meaning of essence: that is, the three patterns of the totally imagined, the other-dependent, and the fully perfected. They truly understand the meaning of no-essence: that is, the three kinds of essential no-essence in marks, arising, and ultimate meaning. They truly understand worldly, conventional meaning: that is, the five stations of learning [which are literature, craftsmanship, medicine, logic, and doctrine]. They truly understand the true meaning of ultimate meaning: that is, the seven emptinesses. Furthermore, in nondiscrimination they separate themselves from all mental fabrication. Arriving at that pure, unitary principle, they abide therein for protracted periods of time. By their vision they objectify the unlimited, unified doctrine and are able to perfect a practice of doctrine in harmony with [that] doctrine. These are the seven characteristics of the purification of discernment."

The Bodhisattva Avalokiteśvara addressed the Buddha and said: "World-honored One, what are the specific actions of these five characteristics [of purification]?"

The Buddha answered the Bodhisattva Avalokiteśvara and said: "Good son, you should understand that these characteristics of purification have five actions. Because they are unattached, the bodhisattvas always exert diligent effort in their present practice of the perfections without laxity. Because they are disinterested, they encompass the causes to avoid laxity in the future. Because they are irreproachable, they are able correctly to practice completely purified and wholly radiant perfections. Because they are nondiscriminative, in their perfection of skillful methods, they speedily attain fullness. Because they are generous, in all their destinies they attain inexhaustibility in regard to all perfections whatsoever and all consequent favorable maturations [of those perfections], and finally reach unexcelled supreme awakening."

707a

The Bodhisattva Avalokiteśvara addressed the Buddha and said: "World-honored One, why are [the bodhisattvas who have mastered] these perfections extensive? Why are they undefiled? Why are they most radiant? Why are they unshakable? Why are they purified?"

The Buddha answered the Bodhisattva Avalokiteśvara and said: "Good son, they are extensive because they are unattached, disinterested, and generous. They are undefiled because they are irreproachable and nondiscriminative. They are radiant because the action of their penetrating understanding is supreme. They are unshakable because they have already entered the state of non-returners. They are purified because they have completed the ten stages and the Buddha stage."

The Bodhisattva Avalokiteśvara addressed the Buddha and said: "World-honored One, why are all the favorable results and maturations of the perfections inexhaustible?"

The Buddha answered the Bodhisattva Avalokiteśvara and said: "Good son, this is so because, dependent one upon the other, these [perfections] are cultivated without interruption."

The Bodhisattva Avalokiteśvara addressed the Buddha and said: "World-honored One, why do the bodhisattvas in faith pursue the perfections, but not the agreeable rewards resulting from them?"

The Buddha answered the Bodhisattva Avalokiteśvara and said: "Good son, there are five reasons. First, it is the perfections [and not their rewards] that are the causes for the highest joy and happiness. Second, it is the perfections that are the causes for the highest benefit for oneself and for others. Third, it is the perfections that are the causes for the maturation of favorable results in future times. Fourth, the perfections are the support for the negation of all defilement. Fifth, the perfections are beyond all change."

The Bodhisattva Avalokiteśvara addressed the Buddha and said: "World-honored One, what are the august qualities of each of these perfections?"

The Buddha answered the Bodhisattva Avalokiteśvara and said: "Good son, you should understand that each of the perfections has four august qualities. First, when one cultivates these perfections correctly, one becomes capable of abandoning their opposites: stinginess, laxity, exasperation, idleness, distractions, and false meanings. Second, when one cultivates them correctly, one becomes capable of [accumulating] the true requisites for unexcelled, supreme awakening. Third, when one cultivates them correctly, even in the present world, one becomes capable of encompassing within oneself benefit for sentient beings. Fourth, when one cultivates them correctly, one becomes capable of attaining inexhaustible, favorable results from their maturation 707b in the future."

The Bodhisattva Avalokiteśvara addressed the Buddha and said: "World-honored One, what is the cause, the result, and the benefit of these perfections?"

The Buddha answered the Bodhisattva Avalokiteśvara and said: "Good son, the cause of these perfections is great compassion; their result is wondrous, favorable maturation and the assisting of sentient beings. The benefit is that fully perfected and expansive great awakening."

The Bodhisattva Avalokiteśvara addressed the Buddha and said: "World-honored One, if the bodhisattvas are endowed with inexhaustible riches, and if they are most compassionate, then how can there be poor sentient beings in this world?"

The Buddha answered the Bodhisattva Avalokiteśvara and said: "Good son, it is because the very actions of sentient beings are sinful. If this were not so, then how would there be poverty in the world, for the bodhisattvas always cherish the mind to benefit others and they are indeed endowed with inexhaustible riches. [There would be no poverty] if sentient beings did not set up obstacles by their own actions. The bodies of hungry ghosts are oppressed by a great thirst, but even if they encounter the waters of the great sea, still they remain parched. This is not the fault of that great sea. It is the fault of the actions of those hungry ghosts themselves! Similarly, the riches to be given by the bodhisattvas, like the sea, are not at fault. Rather, like those hungry ghosts, the force of evil actions deprives [sentient beings] of the fruits [of the bodhisattvas' compassion]."

The Bodhisattva Avalokiteśvara addressed the Buddha and said: "World-honored One, by means of which perfection do the bodhisattvas perceive the essential no-essence of all things?"

The Buddha answered the Bodhisattva Avalokiteśvara and said: "Good son, it is because of the perfection of discernment that they are able to perceive the essential no-essence of all things."

"World-honored One, if it is by means of the perfection of discernment that they are able to perceive the essential no-essence of all things, then why are they not able to perceive the essential essence [of all things]?"

"Good son, I have never taught that one perceives the essential no-essence [of things] by means of their essential essence.[35] Although that essential no-essence is apart from all descriptions and is realized internally, nevertheless one is unable to enunciate it by rejecting all verbal descriptions. Therefore, I explain that it is by means of the perfection of discernment that one is able to perceive the essential no-essence of all things."

The Bodhisattva Avalokiteśvara addressed the Buddha and said: "World-honored One, you have taught about perfection, near perfection, and great perfection. What is perfection? What is near perfection? And what is great perfection?"

707c   The Buddha answered the Bodhisattva Avalokiteśvara and said: "Good son, the bodhisattvas, through unlimited periods of time, cultivate and practice giving, etc., and bring to completion good states, yet there still remain passions. They are not yet capable of vanquishing them but rather are themselves vanquished by them. Perfection refers to the development of such weak commitment during the [initial] stage of practicing commitment. Those bodhisattvas, through further unlimited periods of time, cultivate and practice giving, etc., and gradually increase and bring to completion those good stages. Passions still do make their appearance, but they are able to vanquish them and are not themselves vanquished by them. Near perfection, then, refers to this [stage of development] in the initial stage and above. Those bodhisattvas, during further unlimited periods of time, cultivate and practice giving, etc., develop further increases, and bring to completion good states. No passion now appears at all. Great perfection refers to this [stage of development] in the eighth stage and above."

The Bodhisattva Avalokiteśvara addressed the Buddha and said: "World-honored One, how many varieties of passionate inclinations are to be found in all these stages?"

The Buddha answered the Bodhisattva Avalokiteśvara and said: "Good son, there are three varieties. The first are the passionate inclinations that are removed from their companions. These occur in the first five stages. Why is this so? Good son, all the passions that do not arise connaturally are companions to the arising of connatural passions. Since they no longer are present at the time [of the sixth stage], they are said to be removed from their companions. The second are debilitated passionate inclinations, which appear subtly in the sixth and seventh stages. But if one cultivates their suppression, they will appear no longer. The third are the subtle passionate inclinations found in the eighth stage and above. Herein all passions have been removed and no longer appear. There remains only the support for the obstacle to the knowable."

The Bodhisattva Avalokiteśvara addressed the Buddha and said: "World-honored One, how many varieties of abandoning the weakness of these passionate inclinations are manifested?"

The Buddha answered the Bodhisattva Avalokiteśvara and said: "Good son, there are only two varieties. [The first] is the abandoning of superficial weakness in regard to the first and second [kinds of passionate inclinations]. [The second] is the abandoning of deeper weaknesses in regard to the third [kind of passionate inclination]. The abandonment of the deepest weaknesses I have taught as being the abandonment of all passionate inclinations forever, which consists of the Buddha stage."

The Bodhisattva Avalokiteśvara addressed the Buddha and said: "World-honored One, how many eons must one pass through to be able to abandon these weaknesses?"

708a The Buddha answered the Bodhisattva Avalokiteśvara and said: "Good son, one must pass through three great, incalculable, immeasurable eons. They are incalculable since they cannot be measured in years, months, half-months, whole or half days and nights, instants, moments, or seconds."

The Bodhisattva Avalokiteśvara addressed the Buddha and said: "World-honored One, what are the characteristics, faults, and good qualities of the passions that appear in all these bodhisattva stages?"

The Buddha answered the Bodhisattva Avalokiteśvara and said: "Good son, they are characterized by nondefilement because, from the moment they are fixed in the initial stage, bodhisattvas penetratingly understand the reality realm of all things. Therefore, these passions arise with the full awareness of those bodhisattvas and are not unconscious, and thus they are characterized as undefiled. Bodhisattvas are unable to engender any suffering in their own bodies, and [their passions] are without fault. But they do engender passions so as to be able to sever the causes of suffering for sentient beings. Thus those [passions] have unlimited good qualities."

The Bodhisattva Avalokiteśvara addressed the Buddha and said: "How rare, World-honored One, is that unexcelled, supreme awakening, for it has such great benefit, enabling bodhisattvas to engender [such undefiled, faultless, and good] passions! How wonderful are the good roots of all the word-hearers and solitary enlightened ones! How much greater are these other unlimited virtues [of the bodhisattvas]!"

The Bodhisattva Avalokiteśvara addressed the Buddha and said: "World-honored One, you have taught that the vehicle of the word-hearers and the great vehicle are but a single vehicle. What was your underlying meaning?"

The Buddha answered the Bodhisattva Avalokiteśvara and said: "Good son, in the word-hearers' vehicle I have taught the various essences of all things, the five aggregates, the six internal bases, the six external bases, and suchlike. In the great vehicle I have taught that all those things are identical with the reality realm, with the one principle. Thus I do not teach that these vehicles are different. But some engender false, discriminative ideas by taking the literal sense of my meaning. Some say more [than I intended], some less, but their reasoning in regard to the difference of the vehicles is contradictory. In such fashion they evolve and present their disputations. Such is my underlying meaning in this regard."

Then the World-honored One recited verses to emphasize his meaning:

> The stages, what they encompass, their descriptions, their opposite [vices], their preeminences, the vows they engender, the learnings—all these depend upon the great vehicle preached by Buddha. One who cultivates them well will become awakened. In both the lower and the higher vehicles I have taught the various essences of all things; and again I have taught that all [these essences] are identical with the one principle, for I have preached both the lower vehicle and the higher vehicle. Therefore I teach that there is no differentiation in vehicles. If one discriminates by taking my meaning literally, whether by saying more or less [than I intend], those two [opinions] will be contradictory. In foolishness such understandings will lead to disputes.

At that time the Bodhisattva Avalokiteśvara addressed the Buddha and said: "World-honored One, how should we designate this doctrine on the explication of underlying meaning? How should we revere it?" 708b

97

The Buddha answered the Bodhisattva Avalokiteśvara and said: "Good son, it should be designated as the explicit teaching on the perfections, and you should revere it as such." When this explicit teaching on the perfections was preached, some seventy-five thousand bodhisattvas in that great assembly attained the brilliant concentration of the great bodhisattva vehicle.

Chapter VIII

The Duty Accomplishment of a Tathāgata

At that time the great Bodhisattva Mañjuśrī questioned the Buddha and said: "World-honored One, you have taught about the Dharma body of a Tathāgata. How is this Dharma body to be characterized?"

The Buddha answered the Bodhisattva Mañjuśrī and said: "Good son, the Dharma body of a Tathāgata is characterized as the full perfection of the conversion of support, which one realizes through the practice of the perfections in all the stages. Know that because of two characteristics, it is inconceivable, for it is beyond verbal fabrication and is not a conditioned state. Sentient beings, in contrast, imagine and cling to what is conditioned through verbal fabrications."

"World-honored One, is the conversion of support of the word-hearers and the solitary enlightened ones to be termed 'Dharma body' or not?"

"Good son, it is not to be termed 'Dharma body.'"

"World-honored One, what kind of body should it be called?"

"Good son, it is termed a 'liberation body.' The liberation bodies of all word-hearers and solitary enlightened ones are the equal of all Tathāgatas. But because of the Dharma body, we say that they are different. Because they are different from the Dharma body of all Tathāgatas, all [their good qualities] are different from the unlimited, good qualities of a Tathāgata, which cannot be grasped through reckoning or analogy."

The Bodhisattva Mañjuśrī addressed the Buddha and said: "World-honored One, how should we understand the characteristics of the birth of a Tathāgata?"

The Buddha answered the Bodhisattva Mañjuśrī and said: "Good son, the action of the Transformation body of a Tathāgata arises in many fashions, just as do world realms. It is characterized as being adorned and supported by a host of the good qualities of a Tathāgata. Know that this Transformation body is characterized as having birth, whereas the Dharma body is characterized as not having birth."[36]

708c

The Bodhisattva Mañjuśrī addressed the Buddha and said: "World-honored One, how should we understand the skillful method whereby the Transformation body is manifested [by a Tathāgata]?"

The Buddha answered the Bodhisattva Mañjuśrī and said: "Good son, in all the three thousand vast Buddha lands, in many honorable and high royal households, in many honorable and rich landed households, [those Transformation bodies] enter into the womb, are born, and mature at the same time. They experience desire, leave home, and engage in the practice of asceticism. After abandoning that practice of asceticism, they realize full, supreme awakening. [Such] is the sequence they manifest. This is what is termed the skillful method whereby the Transformation bodies are manifested."[37]

The Bodhisattva Mañjuśrī addressed the Buddha and said: "World-honored One, how many varieties of teaching are supported by those bodies of all the Tathāgatas, by means of which sentient beings already converted, but not yet matured, are led to maturity, and by focusing upon which those already matured are led speedily to attain liberation?"

The Buddha answered the Bodhisattva Mañjuśrī and said: "Good son, in sum, the Tathāgata's teachings number three: scriptures, discipline, and theory."[38]

"World-honored One, what is scripture? What is discipline? What is the matrix [of theory]?"

"Mañjuśrī, wherever I have explained doctrine by relying upon summary schema, that is scripture. It relies upon the fourfold schema, the ninefold schema, or the schema of twenty-nine items.

"The fourfold schema treats the hearing [of doctrine], the refuge [promised by doctrine thus heard], the practice of the study [of doctrine needed to attain that refuge], and [the realization] of awakening.

"The ninefold schema treats the descriptions of sentient beings, their enjoyments, their birth, their subsistence after birth, their defilement and purification, their differences, the act of proclaiming [doctrine], [the doctrine] proclaimed, and the assembling [of sentient beings to hear that doctrine].

"The schema with twenty-nine items addresses [the first four] themes of defilement: the cataloging of actions, their progressive actualization, the power to cause future transmigrations that comes from having conceptualized personality, and the power to cause future transmigrations that comes from having conceptualized things. [The remaining items] relate to purification: the application of memory to the object [of meditation], the diligent zeal therein, the firm abiding of thought [in meditation], the abiding in joy under present conditions, the method of transcending all states of suffering, and the perfect knowledge of these. This last is of three kinds: the perfect knowledge of the support for mistakes, the perfect knowledge of the support for heretical practices among outsiders that depend upon [such mistaken] concepts of sentient beings, and the perfect knowledge of the support for the absence of pride among the orthodox. [The rest of the items are:] the support for meditation, its realization, its cultivation, its becoming stable, its varieties, its objects, the skill to know what has already been abandoned and [to know] what has yet to be abandoned, its distractions, the support for its lack of such distractions, perseverance in the labor and effort to meditate, the preeminent benefit of meditation, its steadfastness, the listing of its holy exercises, the listing of the aids to holy exercises, its penetration to reality, its realization of cessation, the transcendence of its worldly insight

709a

101

into doctrine and discipline over the attainments of the highest insight of all heretics, and the regression that comes from its lack of cultivation, for regression comes from not cultivating [this doctrine] and does not refer to the fault of mistaken views.

"Mañjuśrī, 'discipline' refers to that doctrine about the precepts and the states associated with these precepts that I have explained for word-hearers and bodhisattvas."

"World-honored One, how many aspects are included in the precepts of a bodhisattva?"

"Good son, you should understand that there are seven. The first is instruction in the rules to be received. The second is instruction in the theme of the grave sins. The third is instruction in the theme of the sins against discipline. The fourth is instruction in the nature of sin. The fifth is instruction in the nature of sinlessness. The sixth is instruction in how to be delivered from sin. The seventh is instruction in rejecting the code of discipline.

"Mañjuśrī, the matrix [of theory] refers to my doctrines on analytical exposition, which [explain] eleven kinds of characteristics. They are [as follows]. The first are the characteristics of worldly, conventional [meaning]. The second are the characteristics of ultimate meaning. The third are the characteristics of the objects that are aids to awakening. The fourth are the characteristics of the aspects [of those aids]. The fifth are the characteristics of the essences [of those aids]. The sixth are the characteristics of the results of those [aids]. The seventh are the characteristics of the explanations of the experiencing of those [aids]. The eighth are the characteristics of the things that obstruct those [aids]. The ninth are the characteristics of things which harmonize with those [aids]. The tenth are the characteristics of defects in those [aids]. The eleventh are the characteristics of the excellences of those [aids].

"Understand that the characteristics of worldly, conventional [meaning] are three in number. The first is instruction on persons. The second is instruction on the characteristics of clinging to what is totally imagined. The third is instruction on the activity whereby all things function.

"Understand that the characteristics of ultimate meaning are found in the instruction on the seven kinds of suchness [treated above].

"The characteristics of the objects that are aids to awakening are the teachings on all knowable matters [as treated above].

"The characteristics of aspects are the instructions on the eight methods of investigating, which refer to truth, proposition, faults, qualities, methodology, transmigration, reasoning, and differentiating the general.

709b

"'Truth' refers to the suchness of all things.

"'Proposition' refers to [the questions of whether or not] one can establish a personality; whether or not one can establish the characteristics of clinging to what is totally imagined; whether or not one can establish a direct affirmation, a distinguishing answer, a counter-question, or an answer of silence; and whether one can establish a distinction that separates the underlying meaning from the explicit answer.

"'Faults' refer to all the defiled states that have the errors I have described by means of innumerable different methods.

"'Qualities' refer to all the superior benefits I have described by means of innumerable different methods.

"'Methodology' has six varieties. The first is method in regard to true reality. The second is method in regard to realization. The third is method in regard to teaching. The fourth is method in regard to avoiding the two extremes. The fifth is method in regard to inconceivable discourse. The sixth is method in regard to underlying meaning.

"'Transmigration' refers to the three times [past, present, and future], the three characteristics of the conditioned [arising, abiding, and dying], and the four kinds of causes [that bring this progression about, i.e., direct, antecedent, objective, and dominant].

"'Reasoning' is of four varieties. The first is reasoning from observation. The second is reasoning from occurrence. The third is reasoning from demonstration. The fourth is reasoning from reality. Reasoning from observation means [reasoning] from the causes and conditions that produce conditioned states of being and from the concomitant language [that describes them]. Reasoning from occurrence means [reasoning] from causes and conditions that result in things, that bring them to completion, or that bring them into action once they have arisen. Reasoning from demonstration means [reasoning] from causes and conditions that cause meanings proposed, explained, and defined to be both valid and understood. This reasoning has two varieties: the purified and the impure. In sum, there are five purified reasonings and seven impure reasonings.[39]

"There are five aspects [of reasoning] that are termed purified. The first is characterized as attained through direct insight. The second is characterized as attained through the support of that direct insight. The third is characterized as engendered through various analogies. The fourth is characterized as truly perfected. The fifth is characterized as well-purified teaching.

"That which is characterized as ascertained through direct insight consists in what is known by direct perception in the world, [for example,] that all conditioned states are impermanent, that all conditioned states involve suffering, that all conditioned states are without a self. Such [reasonings] are said to be attained through direct insight.

"That which is characterized as ascertained through the support of direct insight refers to those things that, although not attained through direct insight, can be inferred. Because they can be supported upon the obvious basis of impermanence, which is a matter of direct insight, [one can ascertain that] all conditioned states are instantaneous, that other worlds have sentient beings, that pure and impure actions are never lost. One can ascertain that the various differences among sentient beings depend upon their various actions. One can ascertain that the suffering or the joy of sentient beings is based upon their pure or impure actions. Such [reasonings] are said to be attained through the support of direct insight.

"That which is characterized as engendered through various analogies consists in drawing upon facts commonly known in the

709c

world, such as the birth and death of all conditioned states, [both] internal and external, in order to offer an analogy. It consists in drawing upon commonly known images in the world, such as what it is like to suffer by being born, etc., in order to offer an analogy. It consists in drawing upon commonly known images in the world, such as the absence of mastery, in order to draw an analogy. It consists in drawing upon commonly known examples, such as external prosperity, in order to offer an analogy. Such [logical principles] are said to be characterized as engendered by analogy.

"That which is characterized as truly perfected consists in the ability to definitively establish a proposition as ascertained through direct insight, through the support of that direct insight, and through analogy.[40]

"That which is characterized as well-purified teaching consists in what is taught through omniscience, such as discourse on the final quiescence of cessation. Such [reasonings] are said to be characterized as well-purified teachings. Good son, these five characteristics are the purified logical principles of investigation. Because they are pure, you must cultivate them."

The Bodhisattva Mañjuśrī addressed the Buddha and said: "World-honored One, how many are the characteristics of omniscience?"

The Buddha answered the Bodhisattva Mañjuśrī and said: "Good son, they number five. The first is that if the voice of an omniscient one appears in this world, it will be heard everywhere. The second is that he will be endowed with the thirty-two major qualities. The third is that he will be endowed with the ten powers and be able to sever all the doubts of all sentient beings. The fourth is that he will be endowed with the four fearlessnesses, proclaim the true doctrine, and be irrefutable by any other. The fifth is that in that good doctrine and discipline, he will be able to bring forth the four kinds of monks with the eightfold path. He will engender teachings that will sever the net of doubt, will not be subject to refutation by others, but rather will be able to refute all their heresies. The monks of the holy path will be able to ascertain [those teachings]. Understand that these are the five characteristics of omniscience. Good son, you are to realize that this reasoning from what is well demonstrated, because [based upon] direct insight, inference, and the holy teachings, is termed purified in its five characteristics."

"What then are the seven characteristics that are termed impure?"

"The first is characterized as ascertainable through similarity to other forms. The second is characterized as ascertainable through dissimilarity to other forms. The third is characterized as ascertainable through similarity to all forms. The fourth is characterized as ascertainable through dissimilarity to all forms. The fifth is characterized as ascertainable through dissimilar examples. The sixth is characterized as incomplete. The seventh is characterized as the explanation of impure teachings.

"If something is ascertained through the mental construction of thinking about everything, then that is characterized as ascertainable through similarity to other forms. If the characteristics, natures, actions, cause, result, and differences of things are fixed as all having differences in each of their differing characteristics, this is characterized as ascertainable through dissimilarity to other forms. Good son, if in that which is ascertainable through similarity to other forms and, in its example, the characteristics of all dissimilar forms are included, then its proposition cannot be demonstrated. This is what is said to be characterized as incomplete. If in that which is characterized as ascertainable through dissimilarity to all other forms, and in its example, all similar forms are included, then its proposition cannot be demonstrated. This is also what is said to be characterized as incomplete. Because incomplete, it negates well-understood, purified reasoning. Because impure, it cannot be cultivated. If its characteristics are drawn from dissimilar analogies, if it negates well-purified teaching, know that at base it is impure.

"Reasoning from reality refers to [reasoning] from the reality realm, which abides in all things and supports the nature of things, whether a Tathāgata appears in the world or not.

"[The theoretical matrix on] differentiating the general refers to that final understanding whereby what is at first described generally by a single term is later differentiated and distinguished by many terms.

"[The theoretical teaching on] essences refers to those characteristics of essence I have explained concerning the aids to awakening, which are taken up together with their [different] aspects and objects, such as the stations of mindfulness, etc.

"[The theoretical matrix on] the characteristics of the results [of those aids] consists in the abandonment of all worldly and world-transcendent passions, and in all the worldly and world-transcendent good qualities resultant therefrom.

"[The theoretical matrix on] the characteristics of the explanations of the experiencing of those [aids] consists in first experiencing them through liberation wisdom, and then proclaiming their interpretation for others.

"[The theoretical matrix on] the characteristics of the obstacles to these states consists in all those defiled states that are able to obstruct the practices of the aids to awakening.

"[The theoretical matrix on] the characteristics of that which harmonizes with these [good] states consists in those habits brought about in their regard. 710b

"[The theoretical matrix on] the characteristics injurious to them consists in the excesses of those things that obstruct them.

"[The theoretical matrix on] the characteristics of their preeminent benefit consists in the good qualities of the states harmonious to them."

The Bodhisattva Mañjuśrī addressed the Buddha and said: "World-honored One, you have summarized the meaning of the scripture, discipline, and [theoretical] matrix for the bodhisattvas in a memory formula unknown to heretics. By means of this memory formula unknown to heretics you lead bodhisattvas to penetrate the underlying meaning of what the Tathāgata has preached."

The Buddha addressed the Bodhisattva Mañjuśrī and said: "Good son, hear the truth, for I will summarize for you the meaning of that unique memory formula which leads all bodhisattvas to penetrate the underlying intent of what I have enunciated. Good son, I have preached that both defiled and purified states [of consciousness] lack any purposeful activity whatsoever, and have no personality whatsoever, for everything is apart from becoming. There are no defiled states, for it is not the case that they are first defiled and then purified. There are no purified states, for it is not the case that what is later purified was previously defiled. Since all the common worldlings in their weak bodies cling to things and are passionate in regard to their false views, distinguishing the essence of personalities [one from the other], they imagine an 'I' and a 'mine.' In this false view they say, 'I see,' 'I hear,' 'I smell,' 'I taste,' 'I touch,' 'I know,' 'I eat,' 'I do,' 'I am defiled,' 'I am purified.' In such fashion their perverse efforts increase. But if they knew things as they really are, then they would be able finally to abandon those bodies of weakness, and without any purposeful effort would attain the unconditioned support that does not abide in passion, the highest purity apart from all verbal fabrication, and the unconditioned support without any purposeful effort. Good son, you should understand that this is how I summarize the meaning of the unique memory formula unknown to heretics that summarizes my meaning."

Then the World-honored One recited these verses in order to emphasize his meaning:

> All states, defiled and purified, are without purposeful effort and without personality. Thus I have preached that they are apart from becoming, for defilement and purification admit of no before or after. In their bodies of weakness, [worldlings] are passionate about their views and therefore imagine an "I" and a "mine." It is because of such a delusion that they say "I see," "I eat," "I become," "I am defiled and purified," etc. But if they knew things as they are in reality, then they would be able to abandon those bodies of weakness

and attain that unconditioned support apart from defilement or purification, apart from verbal fabrication, apart from purposeful effort.

At that time the Bodhisattva Mañjuśrī addressed the Buddha and said: "World-honored One, how should one understand the arising of the thinking of all Tathāgatas?"

The Buddha answered the Bodhisattva Mañjuśrī and said: 710c "Good son, a Tathāgata is not to be described as having arisen from mind, thinking, and consciousness. Rather, all Tathāgatas arise from a mental state of effortlessness. You should understand them to be magical creations."

The Bodhisattva Mañjuśrī addressed the Buddha and said: "World-honored One, the Dharma body of all Tathāgatas is apart from all effort. If it is apart from all such effort, then how does it engender any thinking at all?"

The Buddha answered the Bodhisattva Mañjuśrī and said: "Good son, because of the force of the effort whereby they have previously cultivated the wisdom of skillful methods, they do give rise to thinking. It is just as one needs no effort to wake up after a deep, thoughtless sleep, for one awakens because of the force of efforts previously expended. Or it is similar to one who needs no effort to arise from the concentration of stopping [all thought], for he returns [to everyday thinking] because of the force of his previous efforts. Just as one produces thoughts when one leaves sleep or the concentration of stopping [thought], so a Tathāgata produces thoughts because of the force of the wisdom of skillful methods he has previously cultivated."

The Bodhisattva Mañjuśrī addressed the Buddha and said: "World-honored One, [in this case] should the Transformation body of a Tathāgata be described as thinking or not?"

The Buddha answered the Bodhisattva Mañjuśrī and said: "Good son, it can be described neither as thinking nor as not thinking. This is so because it does not have any independent thinking, but it does have thinking dependent upon others."

The Bodhisattva Mañjuśrī addressed the Buddha and said: "World-honored One, is there any difference between the field of a Tathāgata and the sphere of a Tathāgata?"

The Buddha answered the Bodhisattva Mañjuśrī and said: "Good son, the field of a Tathāgata refers to pure Buddha lands adorned with that assembly of incalculable good qualities common to all Tathāgatas. The sphere of a Tathāgata refers to the five different kinds of realms [known by a Tathāgata]: sentient beings, [the surrounding] world, doctrine, discipline, and skillful methods of discipline. This is the difference between the two."

The Bodhisattva Mañjuśrī addressed the Buddha and said: "World-honored One, what are the characteristics of the supreme awakening of a Tathāgata, of his turning of the wheel of doctrine, of his entering into cessation?"

The Buddha answered the Bodhisattva Mañjuśrī and said: "Good son, these three are characterized by nonduality. That is to say, there is no perfect awakening nor any absence of perfect awakening. There is no turning of the wheel of doctrine nor absence of turning the wheel of doctrine. There is no entering into 711a cessation nor absence of entering into cessation. This is so because of the ultimate purity of the Dharma body of Tathāgatas and because of the constant manifestation of the Transformation bodies of Tathāgatas."

The Bodhisattva Mañjuśrī addressed the Buddha and said: "World-honored One, all varieties of sentient beings gain merit in seeing those Transformation bodies, in hearing them and revering them. What kind of causality does a Tathāgata exercise in their regard?"

The Buddha answered the Bodhisattva Mañjuśrī and said: "Good son, the causality of a Tathāgata in their regard is that of a dominant, objective condition, for those Transformation bodies are sustained through the power of the Tathāgatas."

The Bodhisattva Mañjuśrī addressed the Buddha and said: "World-honored One, how is it that, without any effort, the Dharma body of Tathāgatas emits great light for sentient beings and sends forth images of unlimited Transformation bodies, while the liberation bodies of word-hearers and solitary enlightened ones do not do so?"

The Buddha answered the Bodhisattva Mañjuśrī and said: "Good son, it is similar to the fact that the water and fire crystals that come from the disk of the moon and the sun emit a great light without any effort, but other water and fire crystals do not do so, for [the sun and moon crystals are formed] because they are sustained upon the august [creative] powers of sentient beings, because of the dominant force of the actions of sentient beings. Or it is similar to the fact that a *maṇi* jewel crafted by a master craftsman emits the images inscribed upon it, whereas one not so crafted does not. In this manner, therefore, the Dharma body of Tathāgatas, polished and perfected through the intense culti-vation of the wisdom of methods in the unlimited reality realm, is able to emit from itself great light and images of various Transfor-mation bodies. But that does not occur with the liberation bodies of others."

The Bodhisattva Mañjuśrī addressed the Buddha and said: "World-honored One, as you have explained, sentient beings in the world of desire are led to be born among the noble families of warriors and brahmins because they are sustained by the august powers of Tathāgatas and bodhisattvas. In their physical and material well-being they lack nothing. Whether they take on the form of gods in the world of form or in the world of no-form, they are able to attain perfection in their physical and material well-being. World-honored One, what was your underlying intention in this explanation?"

The Buddha answered the Bodhisattva Mañjuśrī and said: "Good son, the august sustaining power [of the doctrine] of Tathāgatas and bodhisattvas, whether in [preaching] the path or the practice [of that path], is capable in all places of leading sen-tient beings to obtain perfection in their physical and material well-being. As appropriate, they preach this path and this prac-tice. Those who are able to, and actually do, correctly cultivate this path and this practice will never lack for such perfection of their physical and material well-being. But for sentient beings who turn away from and reject this path and practice, and harbor thoughts of bitterness or anger, the physical and material [resources] they may have had will dwindle after their lives are over. You should understand from this not only that the august Tathāgatas and bodhisattvas bring about physical and material well-being, but also how the dwindling of the body and riches comes about for sentient beings."

The Bodhisattva Mañjuśrī addressed the Buddha and said: "World-honored One, in all defiled lands and in all pure lands what are those things easy to find? What are those things difficult to find?"

The Buddha answered the Bodhisattva Mañjuśrī and said: "Good son, in defiled lands there are eight things easy to find and two difficult to find. The eight things are heretics, suffering sentient beings, the differences in the rising and falling of houses of high lineage in the world, the doing of evil actions, the breaking of discipline, evil destinies, and shallow commitment. The two things difficult to find are the implementation by bodhisattvas of a high commitment and effort, and the appearance of a Tathāgata in the world. Mañjuśrī, understand that the case is exactly opposite in pure lands."

At that time the Bodhisattva Mañjuśrī addressed the Buddha and said: "World-honored One, how should we designate this doctrinal teaching on explicating mysteries? How should we revere it?"

The Buddha answered the Bodhisattva Mañjuśrī and said: "Good son, this teaching is designated the explicit teaching on the action of the Tathāgata, and you should revere it as such." When this explicit teaching on the duty accomplishment of the Tathāgata was preached in the great assembly, some seventy-five thousand great bodhisattvas all realized the perfected Dharma body.

Notes

1. For this dating of the text, as well as for an account of the technical information about the versions of the text, their composition, etc., see the Introduction to the study by Étienne Lamotte, *Saṃdhinirmocana Sūtra: L'explication des Mystères* (Paris: Adrien Maisonneuve, 1935).

2. These descriptions of the Buddha's qualities and the characteristics of his land became a schema for exegetical reflection; and copious commentarial accounts were written on each phrase, the most detailed of which is the *Buddhabhūmyupadeśa*, extant in both a Tibetan version by Śīlabhadra and an extended Chinese version attributed to Bandhuprabha. Also see the commentary in Chapter 10 of the *Mahāyānasaṃgraha* and its accompanying commentaries.

3. The point is that all things referred to by language lack any essential identity, and are thus empty of defining characteristics. All dualities whereby humans identify things in binary contrasts are thus provisional, not actually real.

4. Verbal teachings are established not to describe reality, but to lead sentient beings toward awakening. Thus, Abhidharma analyses that pretend to identify the essences of the real are rejected as deluded, imaginary constructs like those in a magic show. This critique is extended to all language, now understood as provisional expressions that take their validity only within given contexts and never capture the ultimate truth.

5. Language is provisional precisely because it is tied to webs of images mistakenly seen to contain meaning, while the unconditioned reality has no image. The Yogācāra critique centers in this theme of imagining (*parikalpa*) and its deluded pattern of understanding.

6. Such fabrication (*prapañca*) constructs mental worlds and then mistakes the constructs for pictures of reality itself, enmeshing beings in the transmigratory cycle of birth and death.

[7] Beyond language and words, ultimate meaning finds nothing that might support reasoning, which assumes the validity of words and concepts.

[8] Such final cessation eliminates all fabricated notions of selfhood.

[9] That which is not known by differentiation is not known at all. Thus, ultimate meaning is indescribable because it is not knowable.

[10] All opinions and theories take their validity from their context, in light of the background store of images and words already imprinted onto consciousness. Thus, no viewpoint can attain a final standpoint of ultimate truth. Here, either option of the identity or difference of the marks of ultimate meaning becomes false, if held to the exclusion of the other, in dismissal of the varying contexts in which images and words differ for different persons.

[11] Interpretations are thus deemed to be untrue if put forward through cherished pride which precludes awareness of the one unified taste of the truth of ultimate meaning. Errors in orthopraxis are errors in orthodoxy.

[12] That is to say, purified from the duality fabricated through attachment to that which is imagined.

[13] The entire section is a rejection of the Abhidharma quest for a metaphysics of reality.

[14] The two worlds of form are the worlds of desire and form, which have material forms and in which one appropriates a material body. The third world is that of no-form, wherein there is no such material appropriation.

[15] These are the central themes of Yogācāra: that the mind constructs its realms of meaning through the interplay of conscious activity. See Chapter 2 of the *Mahāyānasaṃgraha*.

[16] The mind itself is thus dependently co-arisen, relying on whatever factors are present. Yogācāra takes the established doctrine of dependent co-arising and understands consciousness as dependently co-arisen.

[17] This passage is often cited as scriptural authority for the *ālaya-vijñāna* in later Yogācāra texts.

[18] This section presents the basic Yogācāra philosophy of conscious functioning, in light of which further topics will be considered in subsequent chapters.

[19] This section on the marks of all things understood by consciousness (*dharmalakṣaṇa*) is the source for the Chinese name for Yogācāra, i.e., Fa-hsiang.

[20] These are the principal concerns of the Prajñāpāramitā scriptures with their theme of the emptiness of all things, here called the no-essence of all things.

[21] The doctrine of no-essence or emptiness is not then a final viewpoint, but an antidote to the imaginative clinging of sentient beings. Yogācāra attempts to embrace the doctrine of emptiness in terms of its understanding of the three patterns of conscious functioning.

[22] The crux of the genesis of delusion is found in language permeations which distort the other-dependent patterns into the imagined pattern of clinging to entities as if they had essential being.

[23] This doctrine equates the one vehicle (*ekayāna*) with the explicit teaching (*nītārtha*) of Yogācāra, while recognizing the reality of the three vehicles (*triyāna*), which are reduced to implicit teaching (*neyārtha*).

[24] This obstacle (*jñeyāvaraṇa*) consists in clinging to the imagined. Its reversal is not only the realization of full perfection, but also the reclamation of the other-dependent pattern of understanding.

[25] Even explicit teaching (*nītārtha*) is empty of essence, for at the end of the day of transmigration, it too is beyond language altogether.

[26] This sentence echoes Nāgārjuna's insistence that all views are empty, not merely incorrect views.

[27] Thus understanding within the other-dependent pattern, recognized as such, supports the validity of conventional, language-formed truths.

[28] This teaching of the three turnings of the wheel is the first Yogācāra application of its philosophy of meaning directly to issues of hermeneutics, and shows perhaps that the basic intent of Yogācāra thought was to develop such a critical philosophy of meaning and interpretation.

[29] After presenting the basic philosophy of Yogācāra in the previous sections, the text turns now to explanations and interpretations of practices central to the tradition, all to be understood within the other-dependent pattern of enlightened consciousness.

[30] Yogācāra thought is also known as "conscious construction only" (*vijñapti-mātratā*), for this is a central theme. There are disputes whether this entails a doctrine of idealism. Clearly the texts do negate the reality of external objects, because they are constructed by consciousness. Perhaps this is but a move toward a critical philosophy of meaning.

[31] An important passage, for here the text rejects the analogy of vision to understanding, and thus theories of naive realism.

[32] These are basic doctrines of early Buddhism. They permeate the Pali Nikāyas and the Chinese Āgamas.

[33] The above analyses, as well as those that follow, are a resurrection of Abhidharma practice, but now brought within the critical theory of Yogācāra, based on the three patterns of consciousness.

[34] An affirmation of the validity of Mādhyamika thought and practice, to which Yogācāra brings its theory of conscious interiority.

[35] This seems to be a negation of the notion of a Buddha essence, such as taught in the Tathāgatagarbha tradition, and in some Yogācāra texts influenced by that tradition.

[36] Note that this text presents a two-body account of the Buddha. In contrast, later Yogācāra texts presented the more familiar three-body doctrine, which included the Enjoyment body along with the Dharma body and the Transformation body.

[37] The pattern for the Transformation body is taken from the narrative account of the life of the historical Buddha Śākyamuni.

[38] That is, the Sutra, the Vinaya, and the Abhidharma. The following item speaks of the matrix, which is the technical language evolved for the task of systematic analyses and interpretation, i.e., the tasks of Abhidharma.

[39] Again note the Yogācāra recovery of reason, put into service for other-dependent Abhidharma.

[40] Ineffability is then no barrier to the performance of true and valid reasoning, and the transcendence of the unconditioned no obstacle to rigorous thought.

Glossary

Abhidharma: A collection of treatises explaining some of the contents of the Buddha's teachings. One of the three divisions (Tripiṭaka) of Buddhist scriptures. The other two are the Sutra (the sermons of the Buddha) and the Vinaya (rules of monastic discipline).

asura: A class of superhuman beings who are in constant conflict with the gods.

dependent co-arising: The doctrine that all things come into being only in dependence upon other things.

emptiness: The quality that all things have of being devoid of independent, real existence. Emptiness is emptiness of *svabhāva,* which is independent being, autonomy, self-nature, etc. The central teaching of Mahayana Buddhism.

five aggregates: The five aggregates that make up sentient beings—(1) form (*rūpa*), (2) sensation (*vedanā*), (3) conception (*saṃjñā*), (4) volition (*saṃskāra*), and (5) consciousness (*vijñāna*).

four holy truths: (1) Life is intrinsically full of suffering; (2) our attachments are the cause of suffering; (3) all suffering can be ended; (4) the way to end suffering is by following the Buddha's eightfold path (i.e., right view, right thought, right speech, right action, right livelihood, right effort, right mindfulness, and right concentration).

gandharva: A class of mythical beings, celestial musicians.

garuḍa: A mythological giant bird.

great vehicle: A form of Buddhism that appeared in India around 100 B.C.E. and which exalts as its religious ideal the bodhisattva, the great being who thoroughly grasps the doctrine of emptiness and is willing to delay his own enlightenment until he can save all sentient beings. Otherwise known as the Mahayana. *See also* Hinayana.

117

Hinayana ("lesser vehicle"): A derogatory term applied by Mahayanists to the various schools of Buddhism that exalt as their ideal the arhat, the religious adept who has transcended all passions. *See also* great vehicle.

hungry ghost: A kind of ghost that always suffers from hunger and thirst.

kiṃnara: A class of mythical beings, either half human and half bird or half human and half horse, who make celestial music.

mahoraga: A class of snake-like mythical beings.

nāga: A serpent deity, a dragon.

non-returner: One who has reached a stage of spiritual quest that frees one from rebirth in the *kāmadhātu,* the world of desire. Such a person is not yet an arhat, and is bound to be born in the upper samsaric world, i.e., in the *rūpadhātu* and *ārūpyadhātu.* Though a non-returner does return to the world, ordinary mortals in the world of desire do not see this return.

solitary enlightened one: A solitary Buddha who had no teacher, does not teach, and lacks universal compassion.

twelvefold conditions: The twelvefold cycle of causes and conditions that make up the human condition, namely: (1) ignorance, (2) volitional activity, (3) consciousness, (4) name and form, (5) the six senses, (6) contact, (7) experience, (8) passion, (9) attachment, (10) existence, (11) rebirth, and (12) decay and death.

word-hearers (*śrāvakas*): Originally, personal disciples of Śākyamuni who heard his teachings; later generally used to mean so-called Hinayana Buddhists. *See also* Hinayana.

yakṣa: A class of demonic beings; human flesh-eaters.

Yogācāra: A Buddhist school, founded in the fourth century C.E., which advocated the doctrine of "mind only" or "conscious construction only."

Bibliography

Chatterjee, Ashok Kumar, ed. *Readings on Yogācāra Buddhism.* Varanasi: Centre of Advanced Study in Philosophy, 1971.

Doboom Tulku, ed. *Mind Only School and Buddhist Logic: A Collection of Seminar Papers.* New Delhi: Tibet House and Aditya Prakashan, 1990.

Lamotte, Étienne, trans. *Saṃdhinirmocana Sutra: L'explication des Mystères.* Paris: Adrien Maisonneuve, 1935.

Masuda, Jiryō. *Der Individualistische Idealismus der Yogācāra-schule: Versuch einer Genetischen Darstellung.* Heidelberg: O. Harrasowitz, 1926.

Powers, John. *Hermeneutics and Tradition in the Samdhinirmocana-sūtra.* Leiden & New York: E. J. Brill, 1993.

Powers, John, trans. *Wisdom of Buddha: The Samdhinirmocana Sūtra.* Berkeley, CA: Dharma Publishing, 1995.

Powers, John. *The Yogācāra School of Buddhism: A Bibliography.* Metuchen, NJ: Scarecrow Press, 1991.

Tripathi, Chhote Lal. *The Problem of Knowledge in Yogācāra Buddhism.* Varanasi: Bharat-Bharati, 1972.

Index

A

Abhidharma 1, 113, 114, 116
Āgamas 116
aggregates 22, 23, 24, 35, 46, 62
  five 60, 97
ālaya-vijñāna (*see also* consciousness, container) 2, 114
angel(s) 27, 31, 36, 39
Āryāvalokiteśvara (*see also*
  Āvalokiteśvara) 9
Asaṅga 3
asura(s) 7
Āvalokiteśvara 77, 79, 80, 82, 83,
  84, 85, 86, 87, 89, 91, 92, 93,
  94, 95, 96, 97
awakening 12, 14, 18, 32, 40, 41,
  50, 51, 52, 60, 70, 72, 75, 76,
  80, 82, 88, 89, 92, 93, 96, 100,
  101, 102, 103, 107, 110, 113
  factors of 22, 23, 24, 35, 47, 61,
  62

B

Bandhuprabha 113
bases (of consciousness) (*see also*
  consciousness) 23, 24, 35
  six external 60, 62, 97
  six internal 60, 62, 97
  twelve 22, 46
Benares 49
birth (*see also* rebirth) 27, 38, 39,
  40, 61, 70, 82, 83, 100, 113
bodhisattva(s) 7, 8, 17, 27, 29, 31,
  32, 33, 40, 41, 49, 50, 51, 52,
  54, 55, 56, 57, 59, 60, 62, 63,
  64, 65, 67, 68, 69, 70, 71, 72,
  74, 76, 77, 78, 82, 83, 84, 85,
  86, 88, 89, 90, 91, 92, 93, 94,
  95, 96, 98, 102, 107, 108, 111,
  112

bodhisattva stage(s) 3, 17, 42, 70,
  71, 72, 77–83, 95, 96, 97, 99
  eleventh (*see also* Buddha stage)
  77, 80
  far-reaching 77, 80
  of expanding light 57, 77, 79
  of flaming wisdom 77, 80
  of invincibility 77, 80
  of presence 77, 80
  of purification 77, 79
  of the doctrine cloud 77, 80
  of utmost joy 57, 77, 79
  of wisdom discernment 77, 80
  ten 77, 79, 80, 82, 83, 92
  unshakable 77, 80
Buddha abode 7, 8
Bhuddabhūmyupadeśa 113
Buddha land(s) 8, 14, 72, 100, 110,
  113
Buddha stage 77, 80, 92, 96

C

cause(s), causal, causality 24, 36,
  40, 57, 62, 68, 83, 86, 91, 92,
  93, 96, 103, 104, 106, 110
centering 1, 3, 23, 51–76
cessation 16, 18, 19, 28, 36, 37, 38,
  40, 41, 43, 44, 45, 48, 49, 50,
  55, 56, 70, 75, 78, 81, 83, 101,
  105, 110, 114
  quiescent 18, 40
  with remainder 74
  without remainder 74, 75
compassion 27, 31, 36, 40, 45, 55,
  82, 83, 88, 93, 94
concentration(s) 47, 52, 53, 54, 55,
  58, 64, 67, 68, 69, 70, 72, 78,
  80, 81, 87, 90, 98, 109

A List of the Volumes of
the BDK English Tripiṭaka
(First Series)

Abbreviations

Ch.:	Chinese
Skt.:	Sanskrit
Jp.:	Japanese
Eng.:	Published title
T.:	Taishō Tripiṭaka

Vol. No.		Title	T. No.
1, 2	*Ch.*	Ch'ang-a-han-ching （長阿含經）	1
	Skt.	Dīrghāgama	
3–8	*Ch.*	Chung-a-han-ching （中阿含經）	26
	Skt.	Madhyamāgama	
9-I	*Ch.*	Ta-ch'eng-pên-shêng-hsin-ti-kuan-ching （大乘本生心地觀經）	159
9-II	*Ch.*	Fo-so-hsing-tsan （佛所行讚）	192
	Skt.	Buddhacarita	
10-I	*Ch.*	Tsa-pao-ts'ang-ching （雜寶藏經）	203
	Eng.	The Storehouse of Sundry Valuables	
10-II	*Ch.*	Fa-chü-p'i-yü-ching （法句譬喩經）	211
	Eng.	The Scriptural Text: Verses of the Doctrine, with Parables	
11-I	*Ch.*	Hsiao-p'in-pan-jo-po-lo-mi-ching （小品般若波羅蜜經）	227
	Skt.	Aṣṭasāhasrikā-prajñāpāramitā-sūtra	
11-II	*Ch.*	Chin-kang-pan-jo-po-lo-mi-ching （金剛般若波羅蜜經）	235
	Skt.	Vajracchedikā-prajñāpāramitā-sūtra	

Vol. No.		Title	T. No.
46-I	*Ch.*	Miao-fa-lien-hua-ching-yu-po-t'i-shê （妙法蓮華經憂波提舍）	1519
	Skt.	Saddharmapuṇḍarīka-upadeśa	
46-II	*Ch.*	Fo-ti-ching-lun （佛地經論）	1530
	Skt.	Buddhabhūmisūtra-śāstra (?)	
46-III	*Ch.*	Shê-ta-ch'eng-lun （攝大乘論）	1593
	Skt.	Mahāyānasaṃgraha	
	Eng.	The Summary of the Great Vehicle	
47	*Ch.*	Shih-chu-p'i-p'o-sha-lun （十住毘婆沙論）	1521
	Skt.	Daśabhūmika-vibhāṣā (?)	
48, 49	*Ch.*	A-p'i-ta-mo-chü-shê-lun （阿毘達磨俱舍論）	1558
	Skt.	Abhidharmakośa-bhāṣya	
50–59	*Ch.*	Yü-ch'ieh-shih-ti-lun （瑜伽師地論）	1579
	Skt.	Yogācārabhūmi	
60-I	*Ch.*	Ch'êng-wei-shih-lun （成唯識論）	1585
	Eng.	Demonstration of Consciousness Only (In Three Texts on Consciousness Only)	
60-II	*Ch.*	Wei-shih-san-shih-lun-sung （唯識三十論頌）	1586
	Skt.	Triṃśikā	
	Eng.	The Thirty Verses on Consciousness Only (In Three Texts on Consciousness Only)	
60-III	*Ch.*	Wei-shih-êrh-shih-lun （唯識二十論）	1590
	Skt.	Viṃśatikā	
	Eng.	The Treatise in Twenty Verses on Consciousness Only (In Three Texts on Consciousness Only)	
61-I	*Ch.*	Chung-lun （中論）	1564
	Skt.	Madhyamaka-śāstra	
61-II	*Ch.*	Pien-chung-pien-lun （辯中邊論）	1600
	Skt.	Madhyāntavibhāga	
61-III	*Ch.*	Ta-ch'eng-ch'êng-yeh-lun （大乘成業論）	1609
	Skt.	Karmasiddhiprakaraṇa	
61-IV	*Ch.*	Yin-ming-ju-chêng-li-lun （因明入正理論）	1630
	Skt.	Nyāyapraveśa	

Vol. No.		Title	T. No.
61-V	Ch.	Chin-kang-chên-lun （金剛針論）	1642
	Skt.	Vajrasūcī	
61-VI	Ch.	Chang-so-chih-lun （彰所知論）	1645
62	Ch.	Ta-ch'eng-chuang-yen-ching-lun（大乘莊嚴經論）	1604
	Skt.	Mahāyānasūtrālaṃkāra	
63-I	Ch.	Chiu-ching-i-ch'eng-pao-hsing-lun	1611
		（究竟一乘寶性論）	
	Skt.	Ratnagotravibhāgamahāyānottaratantra-śāstra	
63-II	Ch.	P'u-t'i-hsing-ching （菩提行經）	1662
	Skt.	Bodhicaryāvatāra	
63-III	Ch.	Chin-kang-ting-yü-ch'ieh-chung-fa-a-nou-to-	1665
		lo-san-miao-san-p'u-t'i-hsin-lun	
		（金剛頂瑜伽中發阿耨多羅三藐三菩提心論）	
63-IV	Ch.	Ta-ch'eng-ch'i-hsin-lun （大乘起信論）	1666
	Skt.	Mahāyānaśraddhotpāda-śāstra (?)	
63-V	Ch.	Na-hsien-pi-ch'iu-ching （那先比丘經）	1670
	Pāli	Milindapañhā	
64	Ch.	Ta-ch'eng-chi-p'u-sa-hsüeh-lun （大乘集菩薩學論）	1636
	Skt.	Śikṣāsamuccaya	
65	Ch.	Shih-mo-ho-yen-lun （釋摩訶衍論）	1688
66-I	Ch.	Pan-jo-po-lo-mi-to-hsin-ching-yu-tsan	1710
		（般若波羅蜜多心經幽贊）	
66-II	Ch.	Kuan-wu-liang-shou-fo-ching-shu	1753
		（觀無量壽佛經疏）	
66-III	Ch.	San-lun-hsüan-i （三論玄義）	1852
66-IV	Ch.	Chao-lun （肇論）	1858
67, 68	Ch.	Miao-fa-lien-hua-ching-hsüan-i	1716
		（妙法蓮華經玄義）	
69	Ch.	Ta-ch'eng-hsüan-lun （大乘玄論）	1853

Vol. No.		Title	T. No.
76-III	*Ch.*	Ma-ming-p'u-sa-ch'uan （馬鳴菩薩傳）	2046
76-IV	*Ch.*	Lung-shu-p'u-sa-ch'uan （龍樹菩薩傳）	2047
76-V	*Ch.*	P'o-sou-p'an-tou-fa-shih-ch'uan （婆藪槃豆法師傳）	2049
76-VI	*Ch.*	Pi-ch'iu-ni-ch'uan （比丘尼傳）	2063
76-VII	*Ch.*	Kao-sêng-fa-hsien-ch'uan （高僧法顯傳）	2085
76-VIII	*Ch.*	Yu-fang-chi-ch'ao: T'ang-ta-ho-shang-tung- chêng-ch'uan（遊方記抄: 唐大和上東征傳）	2089-(7)
77	*Ch.* *Eng.*	Ta-t'ang-ta-tz'ǔ-ên-ssǔ-san-ts'ang-fa-shih- ch'uan （大唐大慈恩寺三藏法師傳） A Biography of the Tripiṭaka Master of the Great Ci'en Monastery of the Great Tang Dynasty	2053
78	*Ch.*	Kao-sêng-ch'uan （高僧傳）	2059
79	*Ch.* *Eng.*	Ta-t'ang-hsi-yü-chi （大唐西域記） The Great Tang Dynasty Record of the Western Regions	2087
80	*Ch.*	Hung-ming-chi （弘明集）	2102
81–92	*Ch.*	Fa-yüan-chu-lin （法苑珠林）	2122
93-I	*Ch.* *Eng.*	Nan-hai-chi-kuei-nei-fa-ch'uan （南海寄歸內法傳） Buddhist Monastic Traditions of Southern Asia	2125
93-II	*Ch.*	Fan-yü-tsa-ming （梵語雑名）	2135
94-I	*Jp.*	Shō-man-gyō-gi-sho （勝鬘經義疏）	2185
94-II	*Jp.*	Yui-ma-kyō-gi-sho （維摩經義疏）	2186
95	*Jp.*	Hok-ke-gi-sho （法華義疏）	2187
96-I	*Jp.*	Han-nya-shin-gyō-hi-ken （般若心經秘鍵）	2203
96-II	*Jp.*	Dai-jō-hos-sō-ken-jin-shō （大乘法相研神章）	2309
96-III	*Jp.*	Kan-jin-kaku-mu-shō （觀心覺夢鈔）	2312

Vol. No.		Title	T. No.
97-I	*Jp.*	Ris-shū-kō-yō （律宗綱要）	2348
	Eng.	The Essentials of the Vinaya Tradition	
97-II	*Jp.*	Ten-dai-hok-ke-shū-gi-shū （天台法華宗義集）	2366
	Eng.	The Collected Teachings of the Tendai Lotus School	
97-III	*Jp.*	Ken-kai-ron （顯戒論）	2376
97-IV	*Jp.*	San-ge-gaku-shō-shiki （山家學生式）	2377
98-I	*Jp.*	Hi-zō-hō-yaku （秘藏寶鑰）	2426
98-II	*Jp.*	Ben-ken-mitsu-ni-kyō-ron （辨顯密二教論）	2427
98-III	*Jp.*	Soku-shin-jō-butsu-gi （即身成佛義）	2428
98-IV	*Jp.*	Shō-ji-jis-sō-gi （聲字實相義）	2429
98-V	*Jp.*	Un-ji-gi （吽字義）	2430
98-VI	*Jp.*	Go-rin-ku-ji-myō-hi-mitsu-shaku （五輪九字明秘密釋）	2514
98-VII	*Jp.*	Mitsu-gon-in-hotsu-ro-san-ge-mon （密嚴院發露懺悔文）	2527
98-VIII	*Jp.*	Kō-zen-go-koku-ron （興禪護國論）	2543
98-IX	*Jp.*	Fu-kan-za-zen-gi （普勸坐禪儀）	2580
99–103	*Jp.*	Shō-bō-gen-zō （正法眼藏）	2582
104-I	*Jp.*	Za-zen-yō-jin-ki （坐禪用心記）	2586
104-II	*Jp.*	Sen-chaku-hon-gan-nen-butsu-shū （選擇本願念佛集）	2608
	Eng.	Senchaku Hongan Nembutsu Shū	
104-III	*Jp.*	Ris-shō-an-koku-ron （立正安國論）	2688
104-IV	*Jp.*	Kai-moku-shō （開目抄）	2689
104-V	*Jp.*	Kan-jin-hon-zon-shō （觀心本尊抄）	2692
104-VI	*Ch.*	Fu-mu-ên-chung-ching （父母恩重經）	2887